language

TIME
LIFE
BOOKS ®

HUMAN BEHAVIOR

language

BY DAVID S. THOMSON
AND THE EDITORS OF TIME-LIFE BOOKS

TIME-LIFE BOOKS, NEW YORK

The Author: David Thomson is a staff editor for
TIME-LIFE BOOKS. A Harvard graduate who also
studied at Columbia and the Sorbonne, he has
taught English and French literature at Harvard,
and English literature at Williams and Columbia.
He is the author of *HST*, a biography of President
Harry S Truman.

General Consultants for Human Behavior:
Robert M. Krauss is Professor of Psychology at
Columbia University. He has taught at Princeton
and Harvard and was Chairman of the Psychology
Department at Rutgers. He is the co-author of
Theories in Social Psychology, edits the *Journal of
Experimental Social Psychology* and contributes
articles to many journals on aspects of human
behavior and social interaction. Professor Krauss
also served as special consultant for this book.

Peter I. Rose, a specialist on racial and ethnic
relations, is Sophia Smith Professor of Sociology
and Anthropology at Smith College and is on the
graduate faculty of the University of Massachusetts.
His books include *They and We*, *The Subject Is
Race* and *Americans from Africa*. Professor Rose
has also taught at Goucher, Wesleyan, Colorado,
Clark, Yale, Amherst, the University of Leicester in
England, Kyoto University in Japan and Flinders
University in Australia.

James W. Fernandez is Chairman of the
Anthropology Department at Dartmouth College.
His research in culture change has taken him to
East, West and South Africa and the Iberian
peninsula. Articles on his field studies have been
widely published in European and American
anthropology journals. He has been president of the
Northeastern Anthropological Association and a
consultant to the Foreign Service Institute.

The Cover: Aboard a Prague bus bearing the label
"výstup" ("exit"), two generations make animated
use of their native tongue.

TIME-LIFE BOOKS

FOUNDER: Henry R. Luce 1898-1967

Editor-in-Chief: Hedley Donovan
Chairman of the Board: Andrew Heiskell
President: James R. Shepley

Vice Chairman: Roy E. Larsen

MANAGING EDITOR: Jerry Korn
Assistant Managing Editors: Ezra Bowen,
David Maness, Martin Mann, A. B. C. Whipple
Planning Director: Oliver E. Allen
Art Director: Sheldon Cotler
Chief of Research: Beatrice T. Dobie
Director of Photography: Melvin L. Scott
Senior Text Editors: Diana Hirsh, William Frankel
Assistant Planning Director: Carlotta Kerwin
Assistant Art Director: Arnold C. Holeywell
Assistant Chief of Research: Myra Mangan

PUBLISHER: Joan D. Manley
General Manager: John D. McSweeney
Business Manager: John Steven Maxwell
Sales Director: Carl G. Jaeger
Promotion Director: Paul R. Stewart
Public Relations Director: Nicholas Benton

HUMAN BEHAVIOR
Editorial Staff for *Language:*
EDITOR: William K. Goolrick
Assistant Editor: Carole Kismaric
Designer: John Martinez
Assistant Designer: Marion Flynn
Staff Writers: Richard Cravens, John Man,
Suzanne Seixas
Chief Researcher: Barbara Ensrud
Researchers: Susan Jonas, Barbara Fleming,
Tonna Gibert, Catherine Ireys, Heidi Sanford,
Jane Sugden

Editorial Production
Production Editor: Douglas B. Graham
Assistant Production Editors:
Gennaro C. Esposito, Feliciano Madrid
Quality Director: Robert L. Young
Assistant Quality Director: James J. Cox
Associate: Serafino J. Cambareri
Copy Staff: Eleanore W. Karsten (chief),
Susan B. Galloway, Georgia Ingersoll,
Florence Keith, Pearl Sverdlin
Picture Department: Dolores A. Littles,
Jessy Faubert
Traffic: Carmen McLellan

A portion of this book was written by Rafael Steinberg. Valuable help was given by the following
departments and individuals of Time Inc.: Editorial Production, Norman Airey; Library,
Benjamin Lightman; Picture Collection, Doris O'Neil; Photographic Laboratory, George Karas;
TIME-LIFE News Service, Murray J. Gart; Correspondents Margot Hapgood and Dorothy Bacon
(London), Ann Natanson and Deborah Sgardello (Rome), Maria Vincenza Aloisi (Paris),
Elisabeth Kraemer (Bonn), S. Chang (Tokyo), Mary Johnson (Stockholm), Sarah Kemezis
(Brussels), Lance Keyworth (Helsinki), Traudl Lessing (Vienna), Sue Masterman (The Hague).

Contents

The Gift of Language

Dr. Samuel Johnson's wife, an old story goes, once burst into a room to find the great writer, usually a most faithful husband, kissing the upstairs maid.

"Mr. Johnson," his wife exclaimed, "I'm surprised!"

"No, Madam," said Johnson, "I am surprised. You are astonished."

This probably apocryphal anecdote contains a kernel of truth about language. Few people in any age have been as conscious as was Dr. Johnson of the words they use or the words they hear. Perhaps only Johnson, compiler of the first great dictionary of the English language, would have recalled under such stressful circumstances that the original meaning of "surprised" is "taken unawares."

It is a general truth, in fact, that few people are normally conscious of the complexity of the language they speak so casually and easily every day of their lives. They just speak, almost entirely unaware of the subtleties of the word choices they are making, of the grammar they are using, of sentence structure or emphasis. Somehow the appropriate words are formed in the mind. Somehow the speech organs—larynx, tongue, teeth, lips—enunciate the words, all with no sense of effort. Sentences roll out without the speaker being in the least conscious of the rules of grammar that govern their structure. Emphasis changes as if by magic as the speaker's voice or word choice indicates the emotional tone of his remarks. All normal humans do this automatically, as if by instinct.

This gift of language is even more remarkable considering that the average adult can pick and choose from a reservoir of some 50,000 words, can make the vocal sounds necessary to articulate them all and can string this wealth of expression in meaningful orders according to the complex rules that govern the use of his native tongue. He can usually come up with the words and phrases that are appropriate to every occasion, enabling him to chatter trivialities or to discuss the ultimate meaning of the universe. When voice or vocabulary fail, he calls on gestures that take the place of words. Such mastery of language is an extraordinary achievement. That all normal humans possess the gift deserves to be called a miracle.

It is language that has made it possible for man to erect the civilizations and master the sciences that make human life what it is today. Language is the primary cause of man's swift and ever-accelerating cultural evolution. The human species has not evolved biologically since long before the Sumerians composed the oldest known epic, *Gilgamesh*, some 4,000 years ago. The Sumerians had heads as capacious and brains as large as man has today. Man has apparently grown a little taller and heavier in the last couple of centuries—doubtless the result of improvements in his diet—but he has hardly evolved in the Darwinian sense since Cro-Magnon types appeared in various parts of the world around 40,000 years ago. But man's ability to communicate information through language—and especially to communicate from generation to generation through writing—has transformed a creature hacking a precarious living out of the earth with stone or bronze tools into the incredible polymath of today, master of technologies and sciences that have launched satellites and put astronauts on the moon, created modern medicine and established the electronic communications networks that bind together the whole world.

It is language as much as anything that makes human behavior human. The brain is the master control center for all activity, but language, to a large extent, governs what the brain does. Language incites anger, elicits love, arouses bravery and triggers cowardice. It incites nations to war, sends their armies to battle and eventually negotiates a peace treaty; it orders temples to be built and canals to be dug; it instills moral precepts and clarifies understanding. In all these ways and many more, language guides and directs the way people act; that is, it influences the course of human behavior. But language is more. It is itself behavior, the expression of the brain's commands.

At the simplest level, speaking is a physical action that is comparable to walking or lifting; countless nerve cells located in the brain and beyond it coordinate muscles that create meaningful vocal signals. In addition, words, spoken with various tones and accents, constitute overt behavior. For example, insulting a man with words is an overt act. Despite the old saw, "Sticks and stones may break my bones but words can never hurt me," verbal abuse can often be as painful as physical abuse. Speech also influences much human behavior: Language establishes human relationships, fitting them to the patterns of society. In the end, language gives each man his identity, proclaiming his homeland, social class, profession and personality. It places him in his world, and it shapes his view of that world.

Language is so essential a part of human nature that every normal human possesses it and no one can be fully human without it. Any interference with the ordinary process of acquiring language in childhood is a severe handicap. Children born deaf suffer a grave disadvantage. Special pains must be taken even with a normal child of deaf parents *(pages 30-41)*. And a child who loses both hearing and sight before learning to talk, as did the writer Helen Keller *(pages 55-58)*, is so cut off from language that only a supreme effort can rescue him from a life of savagery.

Presumably, if to be human is to use language, then the reverse should also be true: To use language is to be human. That is what everyone thought until quite recently. Now scientists are not so sure. For while man is the only creature that naturally makes use of language, he may not be the only one that can learn to do so. Experiments with chimpanzees demonstrate that they can be taught to "talk" to humans and even to one another in ways that seem to transcend the methods of communication ordinarily employed by animals.

All animals communicate with their own kind, even termites, which, if alarmed while gnawing their way through the householder's beams and sills, have three distinct ways to warn one another of danger. They do a curious dance, they make a scratching sound with abdomen and thorax, and they emit chemical odors. Bees also communicate among themselves. A foraging worker bee that discovers a particularly rich treasure-trove of nectar returns to the hive and does a complex dance that helps to tell the other bees how far away the nectar is and in what direction to travel.

More intelligent animals have correspondingly more complicated ways of communicating. Birds have a variety of cries with which they signal to one another. Many species have an alarm cry, for instance, as well as mating calls and a keep-out-of-my-territory signal that is used at mating time. Anybody who has walked in wooded areas in places where crows congregate knows that they have a rich (and from the sound of it, probably profane) vocabulary of raucous cries. And crows, like many other birds, are now known to use regional dialects. One experimenter recorded the distress and assembly calls of a group of crows in France. He then played the tapes to an American group of crows in the state of Maine. He discovered that the down-East birds did not respond; apparently they could not fathom the cries of their French cousins. It

Swinging a bell or banging a drum
to attract attention, the town crier has
carried out the fundamental mission
of language—conveying essential
information—in small European
communities since the 13th Century. In
Rudersdorf, Austria, the village drummer
continues the tradition as he alerts
citizens to the dangers of land
mines, planted in nearby Hungary
during the Cold War years of the 1950s
and washed into Austria by floods.

seems that a crow from Maine has a distinctive accent, just as do the human beings from that part of the world.

Some birds—parrots, mynah birds, ravens and other avian mimics —are such versatile vocalizers that they can reproduce human speech. Their complex vocal equipment enables them to produce a variety of tones and they can be taught to repeat words or phrases with uncanny fidelity. But not even Long John Silver's parrot or Edgar Allen Poe's raven could recombine the sounds to form an original utterance. The mimic birds have not the faintest notion of what they are saying; they merely repeat a pattern of, to them, meaningless sounds. They do not use language but simply play it back like a recorder—it is a technical trick, not a form of communication.

When birds do communicate, their messages are very simple. The same is true of other less-tuneful animals. Many dog lovers will insist that their pets have distinct barks depending on whether they want food, want to go out or are agitated by the presence of a trespasser on the property. Wild chimpanzees, the closest creatures to man in the evolutionary ladder, have a variety of hoots and cries that they use as an alarm system. However, neither birds nor chimps nor dogs can naturally string their sounds together to form meaningful combinations as man can combine sounds in order to form words and sentences. The wild chimpanzee has a sound that indicates the presence of danger, another that signals a young chimp is missing, a third that indicates the presence of food and so on, for a total of 25 different sounds. And yet no chimp has ever strung three of these sounds together to compose a message of greater complexity. Reflecting on the canine inability to combine the sounds of barks and cries into articulate speech, English philosopher Bertrand Russell once remarked, "No matter how eloquently a dog may bark, he cannot tell you that his parents were poor but honest."

By contrast, a speaker of English easily combines and recombines the 45 sounds of the language into meaningful words. The sounds for *n*, *e* and *d* can be combined to form "Ned," "den," "end." The human language with the fewest sounds is Hawaiian with 13—which is 12 fewer than the language of the chimpanzee. Yet out of their 13 sounds Hawaiians have invented a vocabulary that comprises tens of thousands of words. Animals' natural ability to communicate, one psychologist has said, compares to the human communicative power as a dime compares to a million dollars.

If any genius chimps ever learned on their own to use language, they failed to convey it to their young in order to found a line of talking animals. For 1.5 million years or so, language has been an unchallenged monopoly of human beings. As recently as 1968 the pioneering linguist Noam Chomsky could say that only humans could acquire even the "barest rudiments" of language and that such an ability was "quite beyond the capacities of an otherwise intelligent ape." But that was before Allen and Beatrice Gardner, psychological researchers at the University of Nevada, succeeded in teaching an amiable female chimp named Washoe to use sign language. Since that time, as psychologist Roger Brown has put it, man has had the "not especially pleasant feeling . . . that another species is gaining on him. In the study of language, one begins to feel the hot breath of chimpanzee."

Before the Gardners decided to try sign language with Washoe, several experimenters had tried to teach chimpanzees actually to speak. Success was minimal. One husband-and-wife team, Catherine and Keith Hayes, in effect adopted a chimp they called Viki, bringing her up as they would have an infant of their own. They bathed and fed and played with Viki as if she were human and talked with her—or rather, at her—incessantly. The Hayeses kept at this arduous regimen for no less than six years. Finally there was triumph—of a sort. The Hayeses made a movie demonstrating that Viki, with the proper encouragement, could be persuaded to screech out *four words*. This was four more than any previous simian had managed to pronounce, but nevertheless the Viki experiment seemed to prove that Chomsky was right—apes could not really be taught to talk, the "barest rudiments" of language were indeed beyond their grasp.

It was not until the 1960s that such failures were explained. Anatomy, not simply brain power, was the source of the difficulty. It turns out that chimps do not possess the vocal equipment required to articulate words. At birth the human infant's larynx is in the same position as a chimpanzee's, up forward in the throat. But within a few months the base of the child's tongue and his larynx descend downward into his throat, opening up an easy channel for breath and speech sounds. The chimp's larynx remains where it was, making the control of breath needed for speech difficult. In addition, man is blessed with thin but mobile lips, a light jawbone, a nimble tongue—all required for fluent talking and all lacking in the chimpanzee.

When the Gardners saw the Hayeses' rather pathetic film of Viki performing her meager set of utterances, they noticed that the chimp's hands were very active and expressive. They conceived the novel idea of trying to teach a chimp sign language. In 1966 they acquired a year-old chimp from Africa that they named Washoe after the Nevada county where they lived. Washoe slept in a two-and-one-half-room trailer in the Gardner's backyard and spent each day either in the large fenced yard or in their house. During most of Washoe's waking moments the Gardners or their research assistants were around to interact with her in the American Sign Language, "Ameslan," a language of hand gestures developed for deaf people.

After five years of training, Washoe could use some 150 Ameslan signs. More important, she could string two or three of them together to ask for food, to request that the icebox be opened or to express a desire to play. In other words, she could communicate simple thoughts through a form of language. For the first time a subhuman primate had generated phrases and simple sentences. Washoe could not talk, of course, but no linguist would claim that vocalization is a necessary component of language. After all, the deaf "talk" quite adequately with Ameslan. Man's linguistic monopoly seemed to have been broken.

The Gardners' success with Washoe prompted a number of other investigators to try their hand at teaching chimps to communicate with humans. By the mid-1970s at least a dozen chimps were undergoing courses in Ameslan. Among the most optimistic and determined of these experimenters were Herbert Terrace of Columbia University, his collaborator Stephanie LaFarge and an unusually dedicated team of volunteer assistants. As the Hayeses had done a generation earlier, Terrace started with a very young chimp, Nim, and made arrangements to have him brought up exactly like a human child over a long period of time—perhaps 12 or 16 years—teaching him Ameslan at the same speed that a human child would acquire spoken language. Terrace was convinced that if Nim received the beneficial effects of familial love and affection, and associated with companions with whom he could talk, he would continue to enlarge his linguistic capacity for many years.

Terrace began his long-term experiment when Nim was only two weeks old. Nim moved in with Stephanie LaFarge and her large family, including seven affectionate children. The entire family, along with several outside volunteers, started to take courses in Ameslan to prepare themselves to "talk" with Nim whenever he seemed to be in the mood for language lessons. Terrace supplied the family and their volunteer assistants with lists of words that Nim should learn and a timetable for his progress. Nim proved to be extraordinarily affectionate and responsive, and his initial progress in learning to make the signs for simple words like "eat" was gratifyingly rapid.

Terrace expects that as the years pass Nim will cross at least five thresholds of language use. "First, I am going to shout 'Eureka' when

"You"

"feed"

"Booee"

A chat between glib-fingered chimps

The idea that language is unique to man —the one distinction clearly setting him above all other creatures—is crumbling before the chatter of chimpanzees like Booee and Bruno *(above),* who "talk" clearly with their hands. They are among the many who have learned to communicate with what is undeniably a real language: "Ameslan," the American Sign Language for the deaf.

Booee and Bruno were taught 40 gestures, each representing a word, by Roger Fouts of the Institute for Primate Studies, Norman, Oklahoma. They combine the gestures into grammatically correct sentences. Other chimps are even more articulate—one uses 170 words—and some seem to learn sign words from their elders.

In this sequence of pictures, starting at top left, Booee (the chimp to the right) makes the signs that say "You," then "feed" (top right), "Booee" (bottom left). Bruno complies by handing over an orange slice (bottom right).

Nim shows solid evidence of an ability to construct gestural sentences according to grammatical rules. Second, when he starts to use a gestural language to talk about his imagination. Third, when he begins to generate hypotheses about people not present. Fourth, when he begins to discuss the past or future. Fifth, when Nim begins to talk about an inner world—his emotions and dreams."

Whether Nim will prove able to cross these barriers will not be known for years to come. But there is some reason to expect at least partial success. Washoe constructed phrases, if not whole sentences, that often had grammatical English word order, such as "Give Washoe fruit." Sarah, a chimpanzee trained by David Premack of the University of California, has answered questions and has even handled either-or constructions, using a language Premack invented; it depended on arrangements of plastic tokens of different sizes, shapes, colors and textures, which the animal was taught to associate with particular words. One token meant "apple," another stood for the word "and"—and so on. Sarah learned to differentiate and use more than 130 of these plastic "words" and to combine them in the proper order about 75 per cent of the time. Meanwhile Lana, a female chimp at the Yerkes Regional Primate Research Center in Atlanta, Georgia, has learned to punch out simple phrases at the console of a computer whose keys are symbolic "words." Lana has become so accomplished that if she makes a mistake in the sentence she is constructing, she hits the erase button and starts again.

Even if Nim fails to live up to Terrace's hopes, these other chimps have proved that simians can learn at least the rudiments of language —and that therefore the use of language is apparently not unique to the human species. The blow to human pride may not turn out to be quite as serious as all this implies. Chimpanzees seem to have reached the level of human language competence that psychologists call stage I, which is the level attained by the average child between the ages of one and two years. The chimps, like the children, learn the words for familiar objects such as "ball," "food" and "dog." They learn a few action verbs like "eat," "want," "give," "play." They combine them in the same sorts of simple phrases used by young children: "Give ball"; "Want food." But no chimp has really gone much further than that in the use of either sign or computer language. Very young children can answer simple questions, as Sarah seems able to do. Unless Nim proves otherwise as he grows up, chimpanzees are unlikely, according to Roger Brown, to "progress beyond the rudiments that are stage I."

Stage I is not very far considering the extraordinary complexity, the richness, the variability, the subtle shadings and tones that are the hallmark of adult human use of language. The human child outstrips the brightest and most carefully trained chimp by the age of two and a half; after that, he acquires language competence so quickly that by the age of four and a half he is master of the essential structures of his native tongue and can say almost anything he wants. Chimps simply cannot—so far, anyway—match this learning power or even vaguely approximate it. As psychologist Robert Krauss puts it, "The least articulate human is far closer to the greatest masters of prose or verse —say, Shakespeare and Tolstoi—than he is to a chimpanzee. In a land of chimps, any human would rank as a philosopher king."

The superiority language conveys to humans is so obvious that many peoples through history have viewed its use as a form of magic. How this great power came to the human species is part of its mystery. No one knows how language evolved or when, but recent studies permit intriguing guesses.

Cosmonauts Valery Kubasov and Aleksei Leonov greet astronaut Thomas Stafford on the 1975 Apollo-Soyuz mission. To minimize the language problem, the Russian space travelers spoke English to the Americans, and vice versa, on the theory that each would speak more slowly and more accurately in a foreign tongue, thereby minimizing the possibility of dangerous misunderstandings.

A sign language for travelers

For the 200 million people who visit foreign lands each year, finding a baggage claim or rest room can be a problem. And although most international terminals employ symbols as well as words to designate essential services, these substitutes for national languages also vary from country to country.

To help eliminate this confusion of tongues, a new and universal system of symbols has now been designed by the American Institute of Graphic Arts (AIGA). Based on travel signs in Asia, Europe and Australia, the new symbols are being considered for use in 76 countries, including France, Germany, the United Kingdom and the United States. Below and on the facing page is a sampling of the AIGA designs together with previously used emblems.

Information

The question mark—boldly displayed in a circle—was chosen to designate information counters, despite the fact that it is not a universal symbol. AIGA experts felt, however, that it could be learned easily. The two question marks in a square at right and the center symbol were deemed to be too confusing.

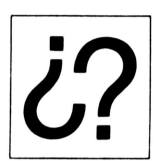

Port Authority of New York and New Jersey

German Airports Association

Hotel Information

The AIGA combined the question mark with a boldly drawn sleeping figure to indicate hotel information. The signs at right and at center were thought to be too poorly rendered to allow their meaning to be sufficiently clear.

Dallas-Fort Worth International Airport

U.S. National Park Service

Currency exchange

Although not completely satisfied with it, AIGA chose the sign at far right for currency information, since it depicted the symbols for major currencies: the dollar, franc, pound and yen. The Canadian sign omitted currency symbols, while the dollar mark that is used in Mexico is not widely recognized.

International Civil Aviation Organization

Mexico Olympic Games 1968

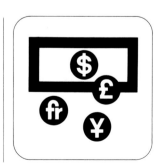

Bar

AIGA opted for the simple martini glass with an olive in it because the other types of glasses depicted here have more than one use. The martini glass is employed only as a bar glass, and the olive makes its purpose unmistakably clear.

Munich Olympic Games 1972

British Airports Authority

Ticket purchase

AIGA preferred the French train tickets at center, but found that tickets vary so in size, shape and complexity that none was fully representative. Instead, the Institute decided on a ticket purchasing situation, choosing the bolder scene at far right over the symbol used in the Dallas-Fort Worth, Texas, airport.

Dallas-Fort Worth
International Airport

International Union of Railways

No smoking

For this symbol, AIGA rejected various signs featuring a cross superimposed on a cigarette, and instead adapted the widely used emblem for prohibition employed on international traffic signs—a circle with a broad diagonal slash.

Osaka Expo 1970

International Union of Railways

19

Many experts believe that some ability to talk was possessed by the first truly human species, *Homo erectus,* which evolved from transitional ape men nearly 1.5 million years ago and did not turn into the presently existing species of man until 300,000 years back. There is no record of the language of these primitive men, of course. The evidence that they could speak lies in their behavior. Some 400,000 years ago in a hilly region in central Spain near the present-day towns of Torralba and Ambrona these ancient men met year after year to hunt elephants in coordinated groups. The remains of the elephants testify to the complexity of the operation. That such a high level of organized activity could be achieved with hoots, grunts and growls is difficult to believe; these people must have been able to talk to one another.

Assuming *Homo erectus* could speak, he was not exactly silver-tongued. As recently as 100,000 years ago, long after *Homo erectus* had become *Homo sapiens,* speech was apparently still limited by physical evolution. The immediate predecessor of modern man, Neanderthal, probably lacked a fully modern pharynx, according to Philip Lieberman, a linguist at the University of Connecticut, and Dr. Edmund S. Crelin, an anatomist at Yale University. With the assistance of a computer, Lieberman and Crelin compared the measurements of modern vocal tracts with those of Neanderthal fossils and concluded that a Neanderthal would have been unable to articulate some of the sounds essential in modern languages: He could not have pronounced the consonants *g* or *k,* nor could he have produced the vowel sounds of such words as "bar," "boo," "beep" and "bought."

Such handicaps had almost certainly disappeared by the time the first modern men—no different in physique or mentality from people of today—appeared about 40,000 years ago. The Cro-Magnons of that era were gifted artists and skillful craftsmen, and there is no reason to doubt that they were equally talented in the use of language.

Hypotheses setting dates for the evolution of language are on firmer ground than those that try to explain how language evolved—not that there has been any dearth of speculation, most of it now ridiculed. One modern linguist, Noah Jacobs of the University of Jerusalem, polished off most of the old theories in a comment on the passage in John Milton's epic poem, *Paradise Lost,* in which Adam, the first man, says: "I named them as they passed, and understood/Their nature; with such knowledge God endued/My sudden apprehension." "What *was* the nature of that 'sudden apprehension?'" asks Jacobs. Was the name that Adam gave to the elephant, for example, intended to sound like the animal's peculiar roar? This theory—that the words of language imitate

In libraries like the Festetics repository of Hungarian writings—one of Europe's largest family collections—language fulfills its purpose of transmitting knowledge. This collection, now part of a public museum, was still privately owned when the photograph above was made in 1938—the lone reader is Prince George-Tassilon-Joseph Festetics.

animal sounds—has been ridiculed as the bowwow theory. Or, Jacobs asks, did names originate from some mystic harmonic ring supposedly emitted by all objects? This theory, derided by modern linguists under the name dingdong, is plainly nonsense since the supposed mystic ring of the canine species is rendered by words as different as "dog" (English), "chien" (French) and "inu" (Japanese).

A third hypothesis, called the yo-heave-ho theory, posits that language originated in rhythmic work chants. Still another, the pooh-pooh theory, is equally far-fetched; language is supposed to have originated in early man's grunts of delight or displeasure. Perhaps the least likely of all is the ta-ta, or wigwag, theory. This holds that Adam's tongue, as Jacobs puts it, "unwittingly reproduced some typical elephantine gesture, an oral replica of the beast's lithe proboscis, the texture of its wrinkled bulk or the swish of its flapping tail." There is no evidence to support any of these theories and much evidence that disproves them. They live today only as amusing relics from the early history of linguistic science.

Most experts now refuse to guess how man first invented language. They believe the invention probably occurred in many different places at various times in the prehistoric past. However, these earliest languages did not grow entirely in isolation, one language being spoken on one side of a tribal boundary line and a completely different language on the other side. Rather, languages influenced one another or intermarried—and produced offspring. Although there remain today some 3,000 languages, 1,000 in Africa alone, they can be grouped into about 70 "families"—a testimony to the human propensity for migrating, intermarrying and borrowing words and ideas. All the languages of Europe, with a few notable exceptions, are clearly related not only to one another, but to such distant tongues as Hindi and Bihari, all of which belong to the Indo-European family *(right)*. The words and grammar are fundamentally similar. The name of the numeral "one," for example, hardly changes its form from English to German, French, Italian or Spanish ("one," "eins," "une," "uno," "uno"). However, there are exceptions. For reasons lost in history, the Hungarians speak a language totally unrelated to those of the neighboring Germans and Slavs; it is a Finno-Ugric language and the word for "one" is "egy."

Despite the fact that linguistic families show obvious resemblances in grammatical structure and even in vocabulary, the individual family members are of course far from identical. An English-speaking person can hardly understand German or French the first time he hears them spoken even though they belong to the same Indo-European group. Like the children of any family, the languages have gone off to make distinct careers of their own. Even related languages have different sound patterns, no one of them more logical or "natural" than any other. All languages, in fact, are simply arbitrary patterns of sound. There is no quality inherent in the animal itself that makes a small rodent a "mouse" in English and a "souris" in French. It seems to an English-speaking person that a dog, well . . . looks like a "dog." But there is no more reason to call it a "dog" than to call it a "Hund" (German), a "perro" (Spanish), a "chien" (French) or a "gou" (Chinese). A dog is a "dog" only because English speakers have tacitly agreed that this pattern of sounds will call to mind the domesticated carnivore *Canis*.

There may or may not be a word for the dog in every one of the world's 3,000 languages, but every one has the words it needs to deal

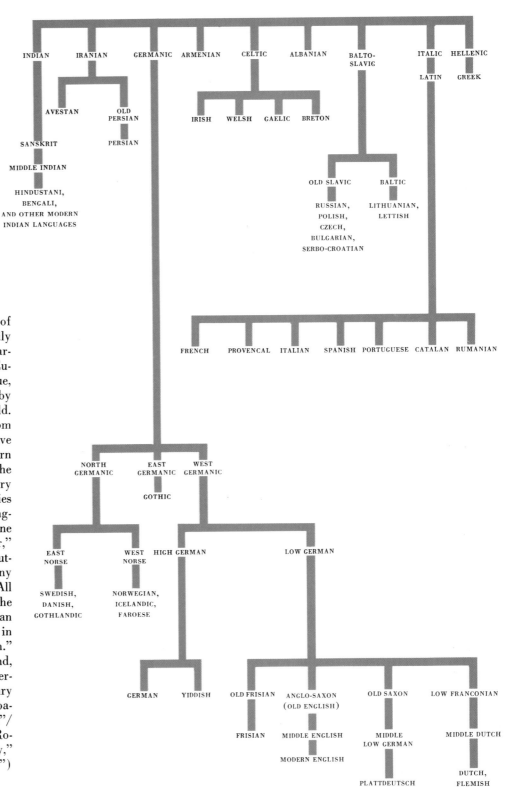

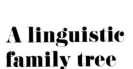

A linguistic family tree

Of the 15 principal language groups of the world, the Indo-European family *(right)* is the most extensive. Its varied tongues—many Indian and all European languages except for Basque, Finnish and Hungarian—are spoken by about half the population of the world.

The whole family is descended from a common ancestor—presumed to have been spoken by tribesmen in Eastern Europe until about 3000 B.C., when the tribe scattered. This common ancestry accounts for the unexpected similarities between such diverse tongues as English, Greek, German and Russian. One example: "mother" in Greek is "mitir," in Italian "madre," in German "Mutter," in Russian "mat'." Even many dissimilarities are only apparent. All Germanic languages tend to replace the original *p* of Romance tongues with an *f*: "fish" in German is "Fisch"; but in Latin "piscis" and in French "poisson."

With comparable shifts in sound, English began evolving from old German dialects about the Fifth Century A.D. The link is still obvious in basic words ("man"/"Mann," "hundred"/ "hundert") but is disguised by Romance terms ("authority," "penalty," "ornament," "comfort" and "pastry") imposed after the Norman Conquest.

23

with the reality its speakers find around them. If a new phenomenon demands a new word, the people will invent one—which is one way languages grow. All 3,000 languages are complex and subtle, capable of the widest varieties and finest shadings of meaning; there is no such thing as a primitive language in use today. The tongue of the Aranda tribesmen of the Australian outback is the equal of French in its flexibility, accuracy and ability to convey both facts and emotional states. So it would seem that no existing language is a crude holdover from the earliest time that man spoke.

Whether languages are as similar as Spanish and Italian or as different as Finnish and the click-filled Khoisan languages of South Africa, they are all articulated through the same physical mechanisms. A number of anatomical parts are involved: throat, vocal cords, pharynx, mouth, nose, teeth, lips and most crucially, tongue. Air is forced up from the lungs past the vocal cords, two elastic membranes that create sound by vibrating like the reed of a clarinet. This sound is then shaped and controlled by all the other parts, which alter the tones and interrupt them to make vowels and consonants. If the air flow is essentially uninterrupted, the result is a vowel. If the air flow is closed off, the result is a consonant. Two major types of consonants are made. Completely blocking the air flow produces a "stop," such as *p* or *g*. Partially blocking air flow produces a turbulent, hissing sound—a "fricative"—such as the English *s* or the German *ch*.

The muscles that control this operation are among the most delicate and precise in the human body. Learning to use these controls properly is a far more impressive muscular feat than, say, learning to skate. In fact, learning to talk is more complex than anything else the human being ever learns. Mysteriously, a child acquires the superdelicate muscle controls requisite for pronouncing his native tongue at an astonishingly early age and as if by magic. But adults seem to have lost the child's natural ability. Any adult who has tried to master the pronunciation of a foreign language can attest to how difficult it is to make the vocal muscles behave in new, unaccustomed ways. Saying a simple, common word like "this" is a lesson in delicate control, which can never be learned by many non-English-speaking adults. The tongue starts between the teeth—not clamped but gently held. The tongue then slides backward as the *th* sound gives way to the *i* sound. Then the tongue moves to the roof of the mouth to sound the hissing, sibilant *s* that closes the word. Meanwhile the breathing apparatus emits a tiny puff that sends the word scudding into the air.

Another example of the degree of precision in breath control required

The inventor of Cherokee writing

SE QUO YAH.

In the early 19th Century, the North American Indians had no written languages of their own, and few Indians could read or write English. They coined the term "talking leaves" to describe the pages of white men's books, and many of them believed that only magic allowed white men to converse with one another by making squiggles on smooth surfaces.

One Indian who thought otherwise was Sequoyah, a Cherokee silversmith born about 1760. Although illiterate, he managed to invent a system for writing down the Cherokee language. Between 1809 and 1821, he devised a syllabary of 86 characters, each symbolizing one sound. The syllabary included many letters from an English book that Sequoyah had acquired. He did not retain their English pronunciations, of course, because he did not know them; instead, he assigned each letter an arbitrary significance. For instance, he decided that *g* should stand for the sound *na*. He also made up some characters of his own. One of them looks like a wishbone and denotes the sound *dla*.

Thousands of Cherokee learned the syllabary, and then, in 1828, the tribe began putting out the first Indian newspaper, *The Cherokee Phoenix*, which was printed both in Sequoyah's language and in English. This journal helped educate the tribe by publishing excerpts from the Bible and from the Cherokee constitution, along with news and articles on farming and other useful topics. Sequoyah's language is still taught in bilingual schools in Oklahoma.

for speech is offered by the brief onomatopoeic word "pop." If the reader holds the palm of his hand in front of his mouth and articulates the word normally, he will find that the first *p* explodes with a little puff of air, but the second *p*, which is made with the lips closed, does not involve any outward breath.

One of the best demonstrations of the oral gymnastics that the tongue, lips and teeth go through is to say over slowly this closing line from a Shakespeare sonnet: "That in black ink my love may still shine bright." Shakespeare is saying that his "shining" love for the person to whom the sonnet is addressed will be preserved to eternity through the poem itself, which is printed, of course, in "black ink." Shakespeare obviously wanted this last line to be read slowly, with emphasis, for he stuffed it with words that require a constant forming and reforming of the vocal apparatus. The reader will find that it is difficult to say the line fast. He will also find, repeating the line very slowly, that the tongue is in constant motion from one word to the next while the lips, open much of the time, have to close to pronounce the *b* and *m* sounds and must be pursed or half open to enunciate "still shine."

The human mastery of language requires an equally astounding ability to make the most subtle distinctions between sounds without ever consciously learning to do so. For example, if an English-speaking person

Belgian police use water cannon to separate Flemish and Walloon students rioting in 1963 over their right to use their native tongues—an incendiary issue in Belgium since 1830, when the country was formed by uniting Dutch-speaking Flanders and French-speaking Wallonia. When the University of Louvain was split along linguistic lines, early in 1963—half Dutch, half French—Dutch-speaking students pressed for complete separation. Rioting ensued, a Belgian government fell, and it was decided to build a separate campus for French-speaking students.

is asked how he forms the plural, he will say "by adding *s*." Indeed, this is the general grammatical rule for written English. But consider how the palate, tongue and associated muscles actually do the job in speech. The plural of "dog" is written as *s*, but when the native speaker says the word it comes out "dog*z*." On the other hand, the plural of "horse" is pronounced something like "hors*is*." Only such plurals as "cat*s*" have the unadulterated *s* sound. Linguists have identified and described an ornate set of rules that govern such variations but the average speaker is totally unconscious of any such rules—he just pronounces these varying plurals correctly.

As great as are the demands placed on the speaker, those placed on the listener are equally difficult. He must perceive the most subtle shades of difference in meaning expressed by the selection of particular words and by the architecture of phrases. Compare "Would you like some coffee?" with "Would you like any coffee?" The questions seem to be identical, but most native users of American English would probably agree that there is a subtle difference between them. The first question —"Would you like some coffee?"—somehow implies that the speaker thinks that very likely the other person would in fact like to have a cup of coffee. The second question implies that the questioner doubts that the other person wants coffee. A tiny word shift, seemingly innocuous, nevertheless alters the meaning of the questions.

More obvious, perhaps, but quite astonishing nonetheless, is the human ability to perceive instantly—again without being consciously aware of any of the rules of grammar that cover such cases—how word order and the introduction of a few little words convert statements into negatives, questions and commands. The sentence "You are going to the movies" can instantly be converted into "You are not going to the movies," "Are you going to the movies?" and "Go to the movies!" Linguists call such changes transformations and it requires pages of charts and diagrams to elucidate them. Yet even a child can usually handle such transformations by the time he enters school.

Not only meaning but social situation may determine the choice of sounds, words and sentences. Take the possible synonyms for the word "woman." They would include "lady," of course, but also less polite and slangy terms such as "chick," "dame" and "broad." There are variations in meaning here, and the word used may be determined at least in part by what the woman in question is like; but the word may also depend on who is talking, on what sort of social gathering he finds himself in, on whether he desires to strike a humorous tone or not. Using the word "broad" at a polite tea party would obviously be a social error, but using the word "lady" in a back-street bar might also constitute an unwise and inappropriate verbal choice.

Such linguistic options—choosing the right sounds and words from the riches that all languages offer—occur frequently in everyone's life. And most people, with only minor hesitations, make appropriate choices most of the time. To make the wrong choice often is to appear crude, or rude, or pompous or ignorant. This is where society and language interact. Every native speaker of a language unconsciously knows and obeys the customs of his language community. Many different levels of speech use are always available, but the speaker's actual options are limited by circumstances.

The subtlety and complexity of this interaction between language and social custom makes it all the more difficult for an adult to master a foreign language. A determined student may take years of instruction and become proficient in enunciating the sounds of the foreign tongue—a most difficult feat in itself—and in its grammar and vocabulary. But unless he has a genius for language he will never appreciate fully the appropriate situations in which to use alternative ways of saying things. He will continually make little mistakes in the social pedigree, so to speak, of his word choices.

Only people brought up in a language community are likely to wholly master such fine points of usage. Children begin learning the differences between levels of their native language early. By the time they reach the age of three or four they know that some words are acceptable at the dinner table while others are definitely *verboten*. At this early age they have already mastered the basics of their mother tongue and begun to appreciate its subtleties.

It is as if all humans were given a fine violin at birth and after a few years of practice and only the most casual lessons could play with the skill of say, Yehudi Menuhin or Igor Oistrakh. At an age when not even the greatest prodigy could have learned the violin, an age when children have great trouble conceptualizing the world around them, they talk clearly. Of all the wonders surrounding language, childhood acquisition is the greatest.

A life without sound

Janos and Elisabeth Schopper, physically and emotionally close to their two-year-old daughter Anita *(right)*, are nonetheless separated from her and the everyday world by a barrier they cannot overcome. Though Anita's hearing is normal, her father and mother are deaf, and their isolation from sounds cuts them off from the many little uses of language most people take for granted. Friends are difficult to find, communications on the job cumbersome, and grocery shopping a problem. But perhaps the Schoppers' greatest concern is the difficulty of bringing up the daughter they dote on.

Born in Hungary, the Schoppers both lost their hearing while very young—he at the age of six months, she at three years—as a result of meningitis, a disease of the brain and spinal cord that often leaves its survivors deaf.

They were educated at schools for the deaf, Janos as a locksmith, Elisabeth as a weaver. They met in 1966, at a convention of the deaf in Budapest, and married a few months later. In April 1970, they emigrated to Germany in search of better work opportunities, and settled near Munich, where Janos found a job *(page 35)*.

Like most people who become deaf before they can hear enough language spoken to master its pronunciation, the Schoppers have some difficulty speaking intelligibly; they must communicate mostly in sign language. They use a mixture of signs plus some spoken words in talking to Anita. At first the words were mainly Hungarian, but they became mixed with German as the Schoppers, with a flexibility characteristic of the deaf, added an adjustment to their new country to those they had already made in a world that takes hearing for granted.

PHOTOGRAPHED BY STEFAN MOSES

Sitting by a TV they bought so that Anita can hear people speaking normally,

Janos and Elisabeth momentarily leave her in wistful isolation as they converse in the sign language that is used by the deaf.

Makeshifts in a silent world

In their effort to lead normal lives the Schoppers depend greatly on special assistance, human and mechanical. When the young couple arrived in Munich, unable to read German and jobless, other members of the deaf community sent them to the city's Social Service for the Deaf, the branch office of a national agency. The social workers at the agency found Janos work, helped the couple settle in their apartment and continue to keep in touch with them. Janos visits the agency often and Elisa-

beth is interviewed at home *(opposite)*.

When the social worker—or any other visitor—presses the button on the Schoppers' front door, special mechanical aids come into play. No bell rings; instead lights go on in every room *(above)*. Until recently, a microphone-and-light device, attached to Anita's crib in their bedroom, listened for baby calls the Schoppers could not hear and alerted them by turning on a bulb. But now Anita can walk to her mother's bed if she needs something.

As the flashing light summons Elisabeth to answer the door, she pauses to caution a pacifier-sucking Anita, warning her with hand signals to stay where she is.

Moving her lips to form words she is making with signs, Elisabeth enlists the social worker's help: she is seeking someone with normal hearing and speech to spend part of each day with Anita so the child can learn to speak clearly.

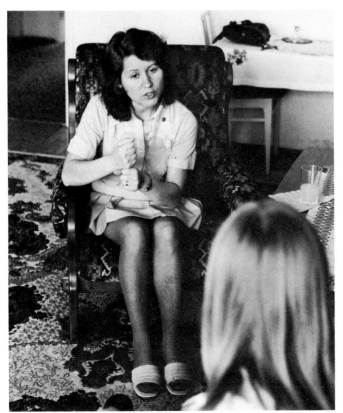

Learning to drive, Janos looks for cars he cannot hear in one of two mirrors in a German training car.

Janos points to some peppers he wants Elisabeth to buy in a supermarket—a self-service store where they can shop without having to talk. The Schoppers are known here, however, and the clerks help if necessary, getting out-of-reach things that are pointed to and filling written orders.

Overcoming everyday handicaps

When a social worker once asked Janos what the Schoppers' greatest problem was, Janos wryly responded that they encounter a new one every day. The routine experiences of ordinary life, from learning to drive a car *(left)* to understanding work instructions *(below)* become tests of perseverance.

The couple's difficulties were compounded in their new country. Janos could not communicate by signs or spoken German well enough to make clear that he was a licensed locksmith, so he took a less-skilled job, putting the final touches on newly renovated cars. The work was strenuous, and Janos met with impatience among some of his speaking colleagues. But he stuck with the job for four years, until he felt proficient enough in his new language to seek more agreeable employment.

Janos' growing self-reliance encouraged him to take driving lessons from a speaking teacher who specializes in instructing the deaf *(opposite)*. Janos, like all deaf pupils, had a hard time gaining confidence in the initial lessons. He was reassured by the statistics: deaf drivers have fewer accidents than those with normal hearing; apparently they compensate for their handicap by developing more proficient vision.

On the job, Janos lip-reads a co-worker's comments, and gestures from habit, though he rarely uses sign language since no one at the plant understands it. Specific instructions for the work that he must do on each car—attaching license plates, washing and polishing—are given to him written down on a sheet of paper.

Elisabeth, who is unable to read aloud
clearly, helps Anita put on a recording of
children's stories. But until a visitor
explained that the record player
had three speeds, Elisabeth played the
records at the wrong speed, and for weeks
Anita heard only unintelligible squeaks.

Anita learns the name of a toy from a babysitter engaged to spend hours every day with her mainly so that she can hear the sounds of normal speech and thus learn to enunciate clearly by imitation.

Bringing up a speaking child

Anita Schopper is one child who is never told that she must stop making so much noise. Her mother is oblivious as she bangs around in her roomful of toys. If she hurts herself she rarely cries —perhaps because she knows that no one will hear her.

Elisabeth is lenient with Anita and also somewhat overanxious. Her concern is understandable. There is always the possibility that her child will suffer an accident out of sight, where Elisabeth cannot learn of it. But a longer-range concern is probably more important: Anita's parents cannot readily teach her to speak. Their own speech is slurred, so she must be prevented from acquiring its defects by imitation. And since they cannot hear her, they cannot correct her. Anita, unlike other children who acquire language automatically, must be taught it consciously.

Anita, hunched between two friends in a close conversation, enjoys playing with neighborhood children. She always runs eagerly to speaking people, possibly because of her increasing awareness of her parents' speech limitations.

Expressing herself with undisguised gusto
while Anita watches, Elisabeth visits
Sieglinde Wehner, a deaf neighbor.
Because of Elisabeth's lingering tendency
to be reserved in her new country, such
visits are not planned but spring up when
the women meet at the store and
Mrs. Wehner invites Elisabeth to stop by.

In the spontaneous camaraderie of the deaf, Janos chats in Munich's train station with a deaf couple the Schoppers met in the station's restaurant. Spotting the couple talking in sign language, the Schoppers asked to join them for lunch, then saw them off on the train.

At ease with friends among the deaf

The Schoppers are unintimidated when they have to deal with people who hear normally, but they do not voluntarily enter into conversation. In the city, they rarely use sign language, to avoid attracting attention.

Such social inhibitions are lacking in the couple's relations with other deaf persons, and they make special efforts to seek out others like themselves. Janos joined two groups that meet regularly in Munich, one consisting of deaf parents, the other a sports club with headquarters in a beer tavern. Elisabeth was slower to become fluent in using sign language for German and was therefore shyer in contacts even with the deaf, but ultimately she too found a new friend *(opposite)*.

To satisfy Anita's urgent desire that he hear the tune played by a music box she has just been given, Janos smiles in feigned appreciation. Anita, while still not fully aware of the meaning of her parents' deafness, early indicated her perception that they lack a sense she enjoys. To get their attention, she learned to touch them on the cheek, and she would also talk more and more loudly to them. When her father read to her, she tried to correct his faulty pronunciation by repeating a word over and over, coaxing him to say it as she does. He never can.

The Art of Talking

A mother and her four-year-old son were having a quiet moment after coming in from the playground. The little boy looked up and burst out affectionately, "Mummy, I *wuv* you!"

"Jimmy, I *wuv* you too," said his mother.

"No, Mummy, not wuv—WUV!"

When the boy's mother mimicked his error, he knew that her pronunciation was wrong, and he tried his best to correct her. Children, in fact, frequently correct their elders' pronunciation and sentence structure at this tender age—and they have some right to. For one of the most remarkable—and significant—facts about language is its mastery by very young children without formal instruction. A two-year-old, like the boy at left learning to articulate words with the help of his cousin, can put together brief sentences. Between the ages of four and five most children grasp the essential grammatical structure and the sound systems of their native language. They can produce a wide variety of grammatical sentences—statements, questions, demands—almost the whole arsenal of linguistic structures that is used by adults. They chatter like magpies. The vocabulary of the very young may still be small and the logic of the utterances may sometimes reveal gaping holes, but the sentences pour out as the child exults in his new-found power to communicate.

Early skill with language is all the more impressive considering the many things that a child cannot do or understand at this age. A preschooler, for example, has only a shaky grasp of such fundamental concepts as cause and effect. He may say that the flowers bring springtime rather than that the spring brings the flowers. As the Swiss psychologist Jean Piaget has pointed out, young children do not comprehend many common-sense ideas. In one of his experiments Piaget found that children do not understand fluidity—they fail to anticipate that the water surface in a jar will remain horizontal if the jar is tilted. Such basic flaws in understanding the world are universal among young children, and yet they have somehow learned to understand and use language.

Realization of the astonishing magnitude of this feat has helped incite something like a revolution in linguistics—an upheaval that threatens the very foundations of broad psychological theories. The leader of this revolution has been Noam Chomsky, professor of linguistics at the Massachusetts Institute of Technology. He suggested in his 1957 book, *Syntactic Structures*, that language is far more complicated than has been generally understood. In subsequent treatises he argued that traditional explanations are inadequate to explain how children learn to talk, a point of view that was shared by other linguists and psychologists. It would seem logical to assume that children learn language the way they learn other things: by imitation. The behaviorist theory of learning would then apply: Children are encouraged to imitate the speech of parents or playmates through reward and punishment —they are rewarded by smiles when they say something right, punished at least with frowns when they are wrong.

This explanation, Chomsky says, cannot apply to language. It is too simplistic. If children only imitated what they had heard their parents say, they would have a small stock of sentences that they could utter and no others. In fact, however, children constantly invent new sentences, things they could not possibly have heard their parents say. Nor could reward and punishment be key factors; children chatter for the fun of it, practicing, experimenting, trying out new words and phrases.

Chomsky insists that children could not learn language so well and so fast unless the human brain was uniquely designed for language. He believes the brain must contain circuits specially set up for language, and those circuits must be genetically determined. Thus some fundamental aspects of language are innate, not learned—they are like the ability to see in three dimensions. Human beings, because they are human, are born with a distinctive capacity to make sounds communicate complex ideas.

If Chomsky is right, some basic ideas about human behavior will have to be altered, and rather drastically. It has been believed that the mind is essentially blank at birth; the human brain comes equipped with a distinctive predisposition for learning but it does not come already equipped with any distinctive knowledge. According to this view, innate behavior—walking, for instance—is limited to activities shared with animals. Anything animals do not do naturally—communication through language is perhaps the most important example—has to be learned through the ordinary process of experimentation and imitation supplemented by reward and punishment. (Even chimps that use language—page 15—do not do so naturally; elaborate human intervention is required.) It is these entrenched ideas, basic to much of psychology, that are now challenged by Chomsky, for he says language is innate, built into every normal human brain.

Chomsky's theory is supported by considerable indirect evidence. But direct proof is difficult. It requires extensive studies analyzing the way children begin to speak in many unrelated languages, and such studies have only now begun to be amassed. Nevertheless, even what is already known about the acquisition of language is impressive, for whether language is innate or not, its development in a child is a fascinating and astonishingly complex process.

The first communications skill the child acquires is not the use of language itself but the use of its basic sounds. Each language has its own repertoire of sounds, different in at least some degree from those used by the native speakers of any other tongue. The human vocal cords, tongue, teeth, lips and larynx can produce an extremely wide variety of different noises. Each language takes advantage of only a small number

A French speech therapist uses a tongue guide and a mirror to show a boy with a speech disability how to place his tongue for the sound of ch—as in "chien."
For children with speech defects or faulty early speech habits, learning to combine the proper lip and tongue movements with the properly controlled exhalation of air from the lungs can be agonizing.

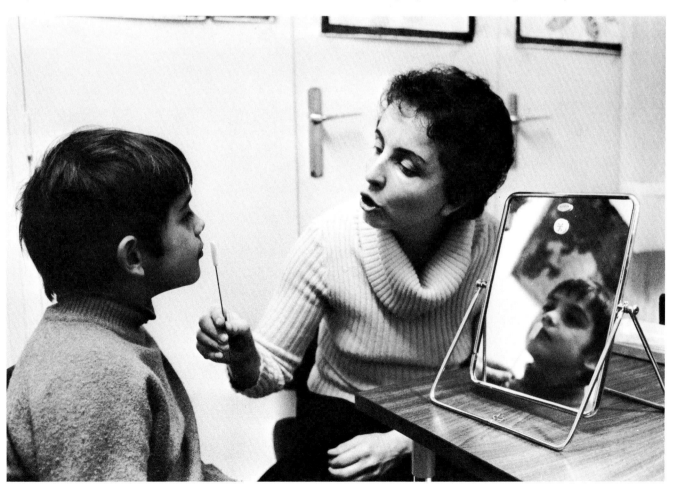

of the anatomically possible sounds, and the child learns these sounds —by experimentation and imitation—very early.

Not right away, of course. The infant in his crib will babble a variety of vocal sounds. Psychologists observing children three months old or so have heard them gurgle and coo in ways characteristic of a dozen languages. The English or French baby naturally makes babbling sounds that belong to German or Russian or Chinese. But very soon—by about the sixth month, according to psychologist James Deese—the child begins to differentiate and to favor some sounds of the language that he will speak. The English or American child will soon stop making the raspy, gargling ch sound that does not occur in English but is common in German—as in the name of the composer Bach. Instead the child will begin to try out the English th sound as in "the," which does not occur in German. The infant tries out many of the multitudinous sounds that the vocal apparatus is equipped to produce but then settles on the limited repertoire exploited by his native language community. Presumably his ear becomes accustomed to the sounds he hears his parents articulate, and he produces them as best he can.

The fundamental sounds that are employed in each language are called phonemes, a word adapted from the Greek for "sound." English has 45 phonemes, Italian has 27, French 35 and Japanese 20. The language containing the greatest number of phonemes—and the greatest variety of sounds—is the Abkhas tongue spoken by a people who live in a section of the U.S.S.R.'s Caucasus Mountains, with 71. The language that has the fewest is Hawaiian, with only 13. The number of phonemes available does not affect the speakers' capacity to communicate information. The riches of meaning possible in all these languages can be constructed out of 13 or 71 phonemes. It is the uniquely human ability to combine and recombine the sounds that man can produce with his vocal organs that makes it possible for him to produce the meaning all languages can convey.

Consider, for example, a few of the three-letter words beginning with p that are meaningful in English: "pit," "pat," "pow," "pop," "pet." A slight vocal adjustment converts the sound of p into the sound of b. The result is another string of meaningful words: "bit," "bat," "bow," "bop," "bet." If the er sound is added to the second list, there are: "bitter," "batter," "bower," "bopper," "better." Obviously, similar permutations and combinations can go on indefinitely until the resulting words fill the 16,500 pages of the *Oxford English Dictionary*.

Languages have many more phonemes than letters. English, with its

45 phonemes, has an alphabet consisting of 26 letters, while the French alphabet has only 25 letters and the Greek 24; a number of the letters of the alphabet have more than one spoken sound. This is especially true of the vowels—the letters *a, e, i, o* and *u* represent not just five sounds in English but 12. The vowel *o*, for example, has three different sounds in the words "cooed," "code" and "cod." Similarly, *a* can be short or long as in "bat" and "bake." Some consonants also do double duty. Two distinct sounds are spelled *th,* as in the thin-sounding word "thin" and the fatter sound of *th* in "that."

The 45 phonemes of English include the stresses and pitches—the rise and fall of the voice—that the native speaker uses to convey his meaning, plus what linguists call a juncture, or pause, and three terminal contours. One terminal contour, for example, is the rising tone the voice makes at the end of a question. The importance of the juncture is demonstrated by two brief phrases that would be identical in sound except for the altered juncture: "white shoes" and "Why choose?"

Stress and pitch are essential to the understanding of many sentences. "I gave the wrist watch to *John*," with the primary stress on John's name, means that it was John and nobody else who received the watch. On the other hand, "I gave the *wrist* watch to John" means John got the wrist watch while somebody else received another sort of timepiece. Many languages rely on pitch far more than English does. The classic example is in Chinese; the word "ma" has three totally different meanings, depending on its pitch contour: "mother," "horse," or "flax."

The phonemes in other languages differ from those in English. French, Italian and Spanish, using virtually the same alphabet, assign different sound values to the same letters. The English *r* is pronounced rather abruptly and with a rather harsh sound, as in "rat." The French and German *r's*, however, are slightly rolled in the throat. They are not as abrupt as the English *r.* The Italian *r* is trilled, the tongue vibrating against the roof of the mouth. In Spanish, *r* gets a long trill as well as a short one. In the Spanish word "pero" ("but") the *r* gets a slight trill, while in "perro" ("dog") the double *r* is differentiated by a longer vibration. So accustomed does the native speaker become to his language's set of sounds that it is extremely difficult for him to learn to produce the sounds of another. English-speaking people are notorious for botching the French *r;* they are simply not accustomed to rolling the sound across the back of the tongue.

The peculiarities of a language's sounds come slowly to a child. At about the age of six months he babbles fewer and fewer of the sounds belonging to the phoneme clusters of other tongues and begins a process

The step ladder of language development

In the early 1960s psychologist Roger Brown and his colleagues at Harvard compiled a clear picture of the language development of three small children between the ages of one and four who were named Eve, Adam and Sarah. Brown and his associates studied the children for nearly two years, sorting out their progress definitively for stages I and II below and tentatively setting forth stages III, IV and V.

The key to the children's progress is the number of morphemes—the smallest meaningful units of sound—they use in each stage. In stage I they averaged from one to two morphemes; after that their utterances increased by an average of half a morpheme with each successive stage, although the children often exceeded the average, and in the final stage the longest utterance had nine morphemes. As they progressed, they learned to form increasingly complex and sophisticated sentences.

In the first stage of language development an 18-month-old baby named Jennifer has reached the point where she can call objects by their correct names and put simple subjects and verbs together.

Stage	Description	Typical sentences
I	In this stage the child starts to put words together, first begins to express the disappearance and the reappearance of objects, differentiates between his and other people's possessions, and constructs simple two- or three-word sentences.	That ball Allgone ball More ball Big ball My ball, Adam ball Adam hit Adam hit ball
II	The child now uses both participles and prepositions; he forms plurals and possessives, uses irregular verbs like the word "broke," and is able to form subject and verb contractions such as "I'm."	I walk*ing*. *In* basket, *on* floor Two ball*s*. It *broke*. Ada*m's* ball. There it *is*. That *a* book. That *the* dog. Adam walk*ed*. He walk*s*. She run*s*. He *does*. She *has*. This *is* going. Tha*t's* book. *I'm* walking.
III	The child begins to make use of the future tense now. He asks questions, leaves out some words, and stresses others—such as the word "does"—for emphasis.	Will Adam go? Does Eve like it? Where did Sarah hide? What did Eve see? Adam can't go. Yes he can. He *does* want to go.
IV	Sentences are longer and more complex in this stage. Relative clauses appear, and two ideas are expressed in the same sentence, such as "You think I can do it."	What is that playing the xylophone? You got a pencil in your bag. I see what you made. I went where your office was. I want her to do it. You think I can do it.
V	In this stage the child makes compound sentences by joining together two independent yet complete ideas such as "We can hear her and we can touch her." He also aptly uses compound verbs, such as "flying and swinging" and compound subjects, such as "John and Jay."	We can hear her and we can touch her. I did this and I did that too. He's flying and swinging. No, you and I had some. John and Jay are Boy Scouts.

psychologists call phonetic drift, enunciating more and more often the phonemes of the language his mother speaks. Even at this early age the vocal apparatus begins to practice and acquire the delicate muscular controls that will be necessary when the child begins to speak—"to wrap his tongue around," as the old phrase goes—the words and sentences of his native language.

The great breakthrough, so anxiously awaited by parents, occurs when the child first speaks words. This usually takes place between the ages of 12 and 18 months, although some children begin earlier while others wait until well after their second birthdays. Late speech does not indicate mental deficiency; the English author Virginia Woolf did not talk until she was three, and Albert Einstein's speech was not fluent even when he was nine years old.

When the child does begin to speak he combines the phonemes he has been practicing into morphemes or into words. Morphemes are the smallest units of meaning. They may be syllables, such as *er*, or they may simply be letters, such as *s*, but their presence changes the meaning of a word. A morpheme can be an entire short, one-syllable word like . . . well, the word "word." Or several morphemes can be combined to form a more complex word. The English word for the machine this book is being written on—"typewriter"—consists of three morphemes, *type* plus *write* plus *er*. Each of these three elements contributes to the meaning of the word. Morphemes include many word endings. One makes the noun "word" into a plural by adding the morpheme *s:* "words." By the addition of the morpheme *y* the noun can be transformed into the adjective "wordy," thus indicating what role the word plays in the sentence.

The earliest morphemes spoken by the child in virtually all languages are those for mother and father—"Mama" and "Dada" in English. The child's words for its parents, it so happens, are much alike in languages around the globe: in Portuguese "mãe" and "pai," in Hebrew "ima" and "aba," in Chinese "mama" and "baba." This similarity is unlikely to result from an innate structure for mother/father sounds. Probably the *m, n, d, p* and *b* consonants are among the easiest ones for the beginning talker of any language to produce.

There are rules for the construction of morphemes; they are more than just an arbitrary collection of phonemes. Just as each language has its own unique sounds, so only certain combinations of these sounds are acceptable. *Blap* is not an English word, except perhaps as a sound effect in a comic strip. But any English-speaking person will recognize that it is a possible combination of sounds. Perhaps it will emerge some day as the name of a new detergent. On the other hand, *sblip* is not a possible combination of sounds in English, although the *sbl* combination can start words in other languages.

All people know the rules for the combining of sounds in their languages—although they are not aware that they know them. Proof of this point was afforded by an ingenious demonstration conducted by Columbia psychologist Robert Krauss. Krauss gave a group of adult subjects a list of words that he had made up. All were nonsense, but some were legitimate English sound clusters, like *blap,* while others were improbabilities like *sblip.* Krauss told his subjects that some of the words were nonsense but that the others were archaic Middle and Early English words that had fallen into disuse; he then asked the subjects to mark the real but archaic words. Nearly everyone correctly marked words that, although they were not English, were possible English sound combinations. Somehow they knew which sounds could have been English words.

Even quite young children already have learned to tell what sounds can be combined. The child's ear is attuned to the morphemes as well as the phonemes of his native tongue by the age of three. An early attempt to say "brother" is often "bubber"—it is not an English word, but the phoneme sequence is possible. Even nursery nonsense rhymes must conform to proper phonemic patterns. The classic nonsense rhyme, Lewis Carroll's "Jabberwocky," employs pseudo words that appear in no dictionary, yet they all sound like possible words, to the point of almost seeming to make sense: " 'Twas brillig, and the slithy toves/Did gyre and gimble in the wabe:/All mimsy were the borogoves,/And the mome raths outgrabe."

Children not only begin to handle the phonemes and morphemes of their language very early but also learn their native language's grammar precociously. Shortly after speaking their first word, children enter what psychologist Roger Brown has called stage I of language use. Before they graduate from this stage they will have begun to communicate with parents and playmates.

In the first part of stage I they begin to enlarge their vocabularies. The first words are virtually all nouns and are the names of things the child has contact with daily, such as "ball," "doggy," "chair" and "lunch." By the age of a year and a half—about the time the child can creep downstairs backward—he has acquired on the average a vocabulary of 50 words. He uses them by themselves to make his wishes known, and by speaking a single word, like "ball," he may perform several functions; that one word may mean "Give me the ball" or "There

Bowwow! or Hau! Hau!

One theory of language, the bowwow theory, holds that words originated as imitations of natural sounds. Linguists reject the idea, though such sounds as animal noises are approximated as closely as each language permits. In Finnish comics dogs bark "Hau! Hau!" Roosters go "Cocoricoooo!" in French cartoons, and gorillas roar with umlauts in German comics.

FINLAND

FRANCE

GERMANY

is the ball" or "Where is the ball?" By the time the child is about two years old—and can turn and walk downstairs—his vocabulary has skyrocketed to between 300 and 600 words. More significantly, the child in this later part of stage I begins to form simple two-word sentences.

The remarkable thing about these early sentences is that they show evidence that the child has developed his own grammar. The child does not talk in random utterances; what he says has structure, although not the structure of the language that his parents speak. The typical early sentence runs "Allgone Daddy," when Daddy has gone off to work, "Allgone ball," when the ball has been lost, and even "Allgone wet," when the child has been toweled dry after a bath.

Using simplified grammar, children in stage I have produced some charming, vivid utterances. Psychologist Martin Braine reports "Allgone sticky" (after washing hands), "Allgone outside" (when the door has been closed and the world outside hidden), "More page" (a plea for another story) and "More car" (a request for a longer ride).

The stripped-down, simplified grammar used by stage I children has been called telegraphic since the child omits the flourishes that adults also leave out when words cost money, that is, when sending a telegram. As Roger Brown points out, only a spendthrift would cable home, "My car has broken down and I have lost my wallet; send money to me at the American Express in Paris." Instead the distressed traveler would cable, "Car broken down; wallet lost; send money American Express Paris." The adult sending such a cable omits the same articles, pronouns, prepositions and auxiliary verbs, the little connector words, that children characteristically omit: "My . . . has . . . and . . . I . . . have . . . my . . . to . . . me . . . at . . . the . . . in." What is left in the telegram are the nouns and verbs that are required to carry the content of the message. The inessentials are omitted. The stage I child leaves out these same inessentials. The child's sentence "See boy" is simply the economical way to say "I see the boy," while "Daddy coat" cuts out the unnecessary words in "That is Daddy's coat."

What is remarkable about telegraphic speech is that it appears to be the same around the globe. Many of the world's languages differ profoundly from English in their grammatical structures, but everywhere children cut out those parts of speech—verb endings, auxiliary verbs, articles and prepositions—that are not essential for getting their message across. One of the telegraphic sentences most commonly used by English-speaking children involves the word "there": "There book," "There car." These sentences are precisely paralleled by a favorite construction used by German children: "Buch da," "Auto da." This

similarity is not surprising, since English and German are closely related. But listen to a child speaking Finnish, which is unrelated to either English or German. When the English child says "More milk" and the German "Mehr Milch," the Finnish child says "Lisää maitoa," which has precisely the same structure and means the same thing.

Children around the globe not only parallel one another's progress in using their native languages but also appear to do so without being coached to any significant degree by their parents. Some parents speak to their children more often than others do or express themselves in sentences that are longer and more grammatically correct. But coaching has little effect on the acquisition of language. Children from highly literate homes and children from illiterate homes alike seem to master the basic structures of their native tongues at about the same speed. Moreover, they achieve much the same fluency. Of course, the child from the more literate home may assemble a vocabulary that is larger and more sophisticated and the grammar he eventually comes to use may more nearly match the polite forms accepted in his society. But all children appear to absorb the principles of the language they hear spoken around them at the same rate.

There are recorded cases of South American orphan children who learn to be fluent in two quite different dialects by the time they are five years old. These orphans, living in less developed nations with few facilities for caring for homeless children, have been forced to beg from infancy in order to survive. They have learned not only the street language common in the slums where they live but also the polite language of the downtown areas where they beg. It appears to be all but impossible to prevent a child from learning the sounds and structures of the language that he hears spoken around him.

It is fortunate that the child does absorb language almost as easily and naturally as he absorbs food. For even in the most polite and cultured homes, children receive far less language instruction than might be expected. Even the most attentive mother seldom does more than help her child expand his phrases into fuller grammatical units. If the child, having crawled into his highchair, comments "Baby highchair," the mother will often echo, "Baby is in the highchair." Or the stage I child may say "Mommy sandwich," and the mother may expand the telegraphic phrase into "Mommy will fix a sandwich" or "That is Mommy's sandwich," whichever response is appropriate to the situation. Roger Brown and his Harvard colleagues found that middle-class mothers in the Harvard community, presumably both literate and attentive to their young, make such phrase expansions about 30 per cent of the time. But this is virtually all the overt language instruction even culturally privileged children receive.

It is not true, of course, that parents never correct the speech of their children; they often do. Parents will correct pronunciation and frequently censure naughty words. But the bulk of this parental coaching is concerned with the substance of the child's communication rather than with its grammatical form. Brown and other psychologists who have studied communication between parents and children report that parents seldom notice, let alone correct, lapses in childish syntax so long as the message the child wants to convey gets through. If a child says, with impeccable grammar, "I hate my brother," he will not be praised for his correct speech but scolded for his antisocial pronouncement. On the other hand, the child will be praised for getting his facts right if, with stripped-down stage I grammar, he says "That horsie, that cow" while pointing to the correct animal. Parents simply do not set themselves the task of teaching language to their young. They concentrate instead on teaching the child facts about his environment, and they let the child learn the language on his own.

A principal mechanism for learning language seems to be experimentation, a constant process of trial and error. Young children are very rarely silent. When Mother is around, the child chatters constantly, asking questions and making observations, providing a running commentary about what is going on even when no words are necessary to accomplish the task at hand. When Daddy comes home he receives the same treatment. But even when nobody is listening, children continue to chatter to themselves. If a child is given crayons and paper, he will often talk to himself about what he is drawing.

This self-teaching of language has been documented by psychologist Ruth Weir, who took down the utterances of her son Anthony as he was falling asleep. Anthony performed pre-sleep sentences. One of his monologues went something like this: "Block . . . yellow block . . . look at the yellow block . . . what color blanket? . . . not the yellow blanket, the white . . . it's not black, it's yellow . . . not yellow, red." He practiced his repertoire of sounds, forming new word combinations, trying out negatives and questions, all by himself.

The rate of progress these self-programed learners achieve is astonishing. When stage I children start to experiment with two-word sentences they create only a few original combinations during the first month. One 18-month-old child observed by Martin Braine created 14. A month later this same child created 10 new experimental word combinations, and in the third month came up with 30 more. In the fourth

continued on page 59

Beautiful and intelligent at seven—but blind, deaf and mute—Helen Keller showed in her face a lack of "mobility, or soul, or something," according to her teacher, Annie Sullivan. The child's face began to be expressive only as she learned to communicate.

An epic struggle to communicate

Learning a language comes almost as naturally as breathing or laughing for most children, but not for those who cannot hear or see. Helen Keller lost both crucial senses before she was two years old, and the story of her gallant struggle to pierce the black silence entrapping her explains much about language—and the human spirit.

Born in a small Alabama town in 1880, Helen was a normal, healthy child when, at 19 months, she had a fever that left her blind and deaf. For the next few years, she could communicate only by gestures and meaningless sounds. Urged on by Alexander Graham Bell, the inventor who spent much of his life assisting the deaf, Helen's father, a prominent Alabama newspaper editor and landowner, employed 21-year-old Annie Sullivan as the child's tutor. She arrived March 3, 1887, beginning an association that lasted almost 50 years.

Sullivan first taught Helen the finger patterns of the manual alphabet for the deaf. Once Helen had associated the patterns with the objects that they spelled, her progress was phenomenal. Working ceaselessly, Helen Keller graduated with honors from Radcliffe College, then devoted the rest of her life to efforts for the blind. By the time of her death in 1968, she had mastered six languages and written 11 books.

The triumph of a gifted teacher

The great breakthrough for Helen Keller occurred one morning when Annie Sullivan held Helen's hand underneath a gushing pump and spelled out the letters *w-a-t-e-r* in the palm of her other hand. "Somehow the mystery of language was revealed to me," Helen later recalled. "I knew then that *w-a-t-e-r* was the wonderful cool something flowing over my hand."

From that moment, she understood that everything had a name. She learned many words that same day—including "door," "open" and "shut." A new world was revealed to her. A teacher named Sarah Fuller showed her how to lip-read by placing Helen's hand over her teacher's mouth and letting her feel its changing shape. She learned to read Braille and to type on both Braille and standard office machines. Renowned for her mastery of language, she eventually became one of the most effective communicators of her time.

Conversing simultaneously with two of her closest friends, Helen communicates with Alexander Graham Bell by means of the manual alphabet, while holding her other hand over Annie Sullivan's mouth to lip-read her teacher's remarks.

First learning to communicate with others, Helen lightly places her palm over her teacher's fingers as they move to spell out letters of the alphabet.

At Radcliffe, Helen Keller typed all her compositions and examinations on a machine adapted for English, French, Greek and math.

Seated in a tree—one of their favorite
places of study—Helen Keller at 24 reads
her teacher's lips as Annie Sullivan
recites from a book. Often, the teacher
and pupil spent most of the day outdoors
—part of Sullivan's informal method,
which was to free Helen from the confines
of a classroom. "All my early lessons,"
Keller wrote in her autobiography, "have
in them the breath of the woods."

month he invented 35 combinations. But then he began to take off. In the fifth month he created 261, in the sixth month 1,050 and in the seventh month 1,100. Children learn language, in short, by creating it themselves, seeking on their own the rules that govern language.

A vivid demonstration that children seek to master the rules that lie behind expression is afforded by the fact that in stages II, III and IV, when children have moved on to more complex sentences using various articles, pronouns and verb tenses, they make a number of telltale mistakes. They overregularize language, applying rules where the rules are not appropriate. Everyone has heard a three-year-old say "Daddy comed home" or "I runned away" or "Daddy taked the book." Far from being mere slips of the tongue, these "errors" reveal something important about the child's knowledge of language. What the child has done is to learn the rule that in English the past tense is normally formed by adding *ed* to the verb. And he has applied this rule to three of the common verbs that do not follow it: "come," "run," "take." Children also frequently say "breaked" rather than "broke," "goed" for "went" and "digged" for "dug."

Children eventually learn the irregular past tenses, but until they do they cling firmly to the regular *ed* form. In an experiment to explore children's misapplication of the regular past tense, Roger Brown and Jean Berko made up the verb "to gling." They showed pictures to children and adults of a man swinging an object around his head and said, "This is a man who knows how to gling. He glings every day. Today he glings. Yesterday he -------." The adults who were questioned almost invariably supplied the missing word as "glang" or "glung," doubtless influenced by the models provided by "rang" and "swung." But the children almost without exception said "glinged."

One little girl about five years old who is quoted by Courtney Cazden in *Developmental Psychology* was especially impervious to attempts to correct her use of the past tense. A dialogue with her mother consequently went like this:

Child: "My teacher holded the baby rabbits and we patted them."
Mother: "Did you say your teacher held the baby rabbits?"
Child: "Yes."
Mother: "What did you say she did?"
Child: "She holded the baby rabbits and we patted them."
Mother: "Did you say she held them tightly?"
Child: "No, she holded them loosely."

Children make other characteristic mistakes that prove they are searching for rules and consistent principles rather than just repeating what they hear their parents and other people say. This happens frequently when children are forming plurals of certain words. The English-speaking child about three years old characteristically goes by the rule, valid in most instances, that the English plural is formed by adding *s*. He says "foots" instead of "feet," "mouses" instead of "mice," "mans" instead of "men," "sheeps" instead of the unchanging plural "sheep." Roger Brown comments, "The important thing about these errors is that they are good errors. Good, in the sense that each one is perfectly intelligible, a quite reasonable overextension of certain regularities that do exist in English and apply in most cases." Brown goes on to look at another characteristic childhood error, "hisself." Similar pronouns just add "self" to the basic possessive pronoun: "your" becomes "yourself," "my" becomes "myself." But this rule does not apply to "his." "Rather," as Brown says, "for obscure historical reasons, the 'right' form, the form belonging to the dialect of the socially dominant speakers, is *himself*. In creating *hisself*, as every normal English-speaking child I have heard does, the child might be said to improve on the language, making it more simply rule-governed than it actually is. He irons out an unnecessary inconsistency. A form like *himself*, which actually has to be memorized as such, and cannot be constructed by rule as the others can, is a nuisance."

In the later stages of a child's language development, he starts not only to apply (and misapply) rules but also to use many of the auxiliary words he left out of his earlier two-word, stage I expressions. He starts using articles, such as "a" and "the" as well as pronouns—"he," "me," "it." And he runs into other tangled linguistic thickets.

One of the most tangled problems that the child confronts is the various classes of nouns. First of all there are what linguists call count nouns, which take the article in the singular, for example, "a coat," "a dog," "a cup." Then there are nouns like "celery" or "dirt." No adult would say "a celery" or "a dirt" because these are mass nouns and take the article "the." In addition, there are proper nouns such as people's names. No adult would say "a Robert"—these nouns take no article at all. All this appears elementary to an adult, who is long accustomed to obeying certain rules even though he probably cannot recite them. But children must learn these complexities, and they must learn them by themselves since no parent ever sits down with a child and explains that there are three classes of nouns, or systematically drills the child in the use of the proper articles.

In the same way children eventually learn on their own to form the tricky devices called tag questions. A sample tag question might run,

Six blocks, each painted with a different abstract design, were used to evaluate the ability of four- and five-year-olds to describe unfamiliar shapes to other children, who were hidden behind screens trying to pick out matching blocks. But youngsters this age drew on words that related only to their own experiences and were no help to the other children. One tot described the form at lower right as looking like "Mommy's hat."

"John is going to the movies, isn't he?" The tag is the phrase "isn't he," which converts a declarative sentence into a question. The use of tags sounds simple until the variety and complexity of such questions are considered. Roger Brown lists a few of the tag questions that one child produced before he reached the age of five:

"Ursula's my sister, isn't she?"

"I made a mistake, didn't I?"

"The girls were running, weren't they?"

"He can't beat me, can he?"

"He doesn't know what to do, does he?"

Every tag in the list is different. For tags must change as the main part of the sentence changes and they must always do three things. The pronoun has to match in person, number and gender the subject of the main part of the sentence. A girl, Ursula, is the subject of the first sentence above and so the pronoun in the tag must be feminine, "she." In the third sentence two people are involved, so the pronoun must be plural, "they." Also, the verb in the tag must match the verb in the main phrase in tense, person and number. Finally, the verb in the tag must reverse the form of the verb in the main part of the sentence. The main phrase of "Ursula's my sister, isn't she?" is positive: It asserts that Ursula is indeed the boy's sister. Therefore the verb in the tag must be negative, "isn't." In contrast, the verb in "He can't beat me" is negative, so the tag's verb must be positive, "can."

It is immediately clear from these few examples that tag questions, which are so easily handled by adult speakers, are in fact full of grammatical booby traps. Brown's admirably concise summation of the grammatical rules that are involved in using tag questions takes some 88 lines of small, compact type. Somehow the preschool child, who has never heard of any of the relevant grammatical rules, masters this complex process.

Tags apparently are among the last things the child learns to manage as he approaches mastery of his native language. To say that by the age of four and a half the average child has "mastered language" does not mean that children are all budding Shakespeares or even that they always manage to communicate what they want or feel or know. There are many breakdowns in communication between child and parent and between the child and other children. The child's vocabulary is as yet far from sophisticated and he cannot communicate many things because he is not old enough to understand many concepts. For all his precocious ability to speak, he is still far from achieving an adult's understanding of the reality around him.

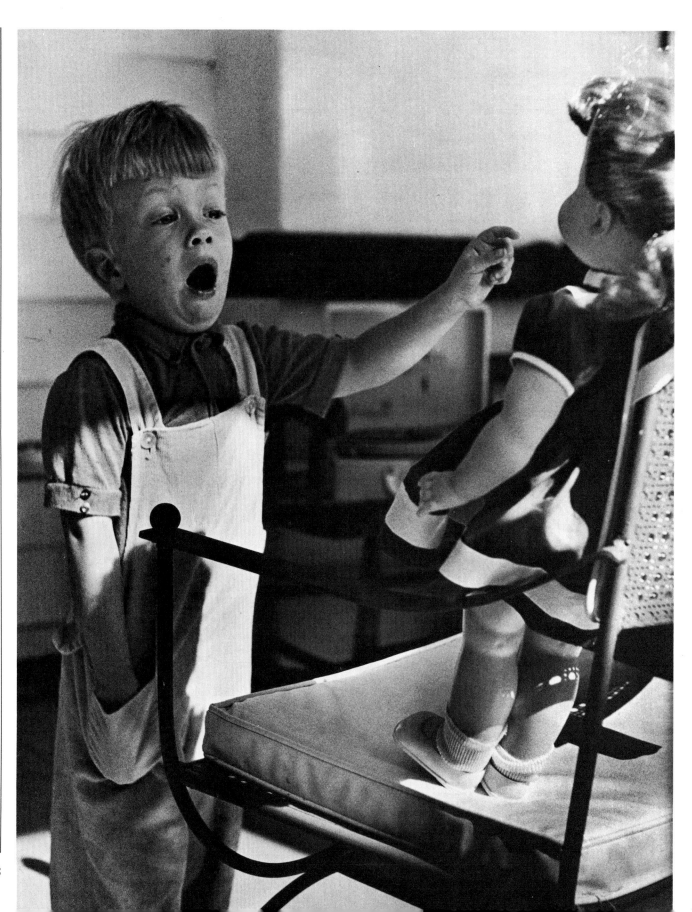

The doll is a passive listener in this preschooler's make-believe conversation. At this stage, the child has not fully learned to enter into the give-and-take of a normal conversation in which the roles of speaker and listener are assumed alternately and matters of mutual interest are exchanged. His speech is still primarily egocentric, but he has begun to feel the need for a listener and pretends the doll shares his own concerns.

An important obstacle to the child's ability to communicate is what Jean Piaget dubbed egocentrism. By this he does not mean that every child is a little monster of egotism; rather Piaget means that a young child characteristically talks without taking much thought to his listener. If what the child says is clear to him, he assumes that it will be clear to the person listening—and of course this is not always so. The child does not put himself in his listener's place; he does not tailor his utterances to common experiences.

The clearest and simplest demonstration of this egocentrism is an experiment—essentially a simple game—invented by psychologists Robert Krauss and Sam Glucksberg. Two children were seated at a table, with a screen between them so they could not see each other. Each child had a matching collection of six blocks, and each of the blocks had a distinctive drawing on it. The drawings were abstract, that is, they did not show recognizable things like hats or men or balls or dogs, but each was quite different and distinguishable from all the others. The child on one side of the screen was to pick up the blocks one at a time and describe the drawings on them as best he could. The other child was to select from his store of blocks the block that matched the one that had been described.

The very young children did wretchedly at the game. Complete success was not attained until 12- and 13-year-old children were tested. The reason for the failures was the idiosyncratic way the children described the drawings. One little boy, trying to describe a drawing that was mostly wavy lines, said simply, "the sheet." To him the wavy lines looked the way his mussed bed sheet looked when he got out of his bed in the morning. But the other child, trying to decode this utterance, was entirely at a loss as to which of the blocks to pick up. The description was egocentric; it seemed perfectly adequate to the boy who said it —that is what his bed looked like. But it was meaningless to the other child, who could not decode such a private, personal description. Similar private descriptions were used by all the children, who said things like "my mother's dress," "the wallpaper at home" and so on, all unintelligible to other children who had never seen the dress or wallpaper in question.

The older children, like the adults who also took the test, were far more careful to give descriptions that the other person could easily recognize. One 13-year-old, after puzzling for a while over how to describe one drawing, asked the experimenter if the listening child was a Roman Catholic. When the experimenter said "yes," the 13-year-old described the block as resembling "that thing the priest uses in the Mass." This

boy took the trouble to determine whether the other child shared his frame of reference—familiarity with the Mass—before using the description. Adults also endeavored to provide descriptions that would be intelligible to the listeners, and for the most part they avoided private or obscure references.

As this experiment with the blocks illustrates, young children lack the cognitive skill or knowledge that is needed to take into account the perspective of another person. That is one reason why parents often find the pronouncements of their young puzzling and have to question them over and over again for enlightenment. The child can speak perfectly clearly in one sense; the sentences are adequately enunciated and comprehensibly structured. But he lacks the ability to detach himself from his own point of view, to explain all of the factors that need explaining.

The child of four or five plainly is not a polished, precise and dazzlingly eloquent communicator—although children occasionally come up with remarkably colorful and vivid sentences. Egocentrism and simple gaps in the child's understanding often prevent him from getting his message across. But it is also incontestible that the four- to five-year-old has already learned most of the underlying grammatical rules of his native language. His mastery of these rules is attested most vividly by his ability to formulate those extremely difficult structures called tag questions. Moreover he is capable of understanding a seemingly infinite number of sentences that have never been spoken to him before, and he can construct vast numbers of original sentences he has never heard.

Remarkable as this achievement is, it can be understood largely—but not entirely—as the result of a complex learning process, in which children imitate others, experiment and slowly perfect their skills. Even the fact that language is acquired spontaneously, without teaching, might seem to be accounted for by the human predisposition to collect and organize knowledge. Human beings are notoriously curious. And more than any animal, they fit together what they find out, organizing their perceptions into orderly systems. Once a set of rules—a language structure—is established, it can be applied to extend knowledge and skill in order to satisfy the human drive to communicate. In this way a child could make up grammatically correct sentences he has never heard—he need not imitate them; he can simply create them to fit rules he has already derived.

Yet language is so complex that nothing now known about the learning process seems sufficient to explain what the child does in so short a time. Noam Chomsky argues that language exists on two levels, the sur-

65

face syntax of the sentence and something he calls deep structure—the fundamental, underlying meaning of the sentence. The two sentences "John is eager to please" and "John is easy to please" have precisely the same surface syntax. But their deep structures are different. In the first, John is obviously the active party, "eager to please" other people. In the second sentence John is passive—others try to please him. That the two sentences are different in a fundamental way can be demonstrated by trying to turn them around. "It is easy to please John" makes sense, but trying to convert the other sentence into its passive form—"It is eager to please John"—produces nonsense. Chomsky contends that all speakers of a language unconsciously understand such deep structures—the real, underlying meanings—of the sentences that they speak or hear or read. That is why people can speak their language as flexibly as they do and why they are able to understand the intended meanings of the multitudes of sentences they hear—in short, why human communication succeeds.

If this unconscious understanding of deep structure extended only to the speaker's native tongue, it would have to be a skill learned somehow after birth, not an innate quality of the human brain, as Chomsky maintains. Chomsky's theory transcends the limits of individual languages; it must apply around the globe. It requires the existence of a kind of universal grammar—a scheme for organizing spoken ideas that is the same in Swahili, Hawaiian, Hindi, Hungarian and every other of the 3,000 tongues in the world.

The universal grammar has yet to be found. But hints of it appear in the telegraphic speech used by young children during stage I of language acquisition. Some of the most convincing evidence is that compiled by Melissa Bowerman of the University of Kansas. She compared the early speech of children acquiring four very different languages—American children, Finnish children, Samoan children and the children of east-central Africa who speak the Luo language. The four tongues are, as far as anyone can tell, entirely unrelated. Bowerman discovered that the stage I telegraphic sentences children constructed in the four languages were much alike despite the wide differences in the grammatical structures of the four languages when they are spoken by adults. She concluded, in fact, that it would be possible, although nobody has done it as yet, to construct a single grammar adequately describing how children in all four of these speech communities construct their early utterances.

The debate over Chomsky's theories will doubtless continue for a long time. But more and more influential psychologists, such as Roger

On the blackboard:

poucette

5 filles   est

une jolie petite fille,

6 garçons   née dans

0   une fleur

A girl in a French primary school parses a sentence, "Poucette is a pretty little girl, born in a flower," as part of a lesson in the formal rules of grammar—rules she already follows in her speech even if she cannot yet explain what they are. By the age of four and a half, most children have acquired an intuitive knowledge of grammar without any special training.

Brown, find themselves forced to agree that language obeys inner laws too complex for a child, or adult, to learn in the way other habits are learned. "One is compelled to assume that the human brain," says Brown, "is programmed to extract from whatever sentences are heard underlying rules of construction that operate automatically and are only known implicitly."

The child not only naturally grasps the rules of sentence structure of the language he hears, he also uses this knowledge frequently to construct wonderfully vivid and succinct expressions, delighting the ear and the imagination. Not long ago a group of five-year-olds were traveling with their teacher on a bus to New York's Central Park Zoo. The talk suddenly swung around to the topic of inoculations for chicken pox. First one child and then another loudly announced that he or she had been immunized, had had a shot. One little girl announced with sublime economy: "I've been chicken shot." Seldom have two nouns been transformed into one verb more felicitously, or the deep structure of a sentence been combined with vivid language more effectively.

A Mute Eloquence

When Fiorello La Guardia was Mayor of New York in the 1930s and '40s, any observant native of the city could tell which language the "Little Flower" was speaking by watching his gestures. La Guardia was of mixed Jewish and Italian ancestry, and he was fluent in Italian and Yiddish as well as in New York-flavored English. When he was speaking Italian to an Italo-American audience, the Mayor used gestures that were broad and sweeping, the characteristic expansive arm-waving of the southern part of Italy. When he spoke in Yiddish, La Guardia employed the forearm chop that is common among East European Jews. His English, although rich and racy, was accompanied by the softer, less emphatic movements that English speakers learn even as they absorb the spoken language.

La Guardia's gestures were as revealing as his spoken words because everyone, as he grows up, learns not only to speak his native tongue, but also to use the varied and subtle gestures that accompany his culture's speech—or sometimes take the place of words. Everybody gestures while he speaks, and communicates not only with hands and arms but also with face, touch, stance and even—like the English soccer player at left—with his whole body. All these signals, whether vocal or not, are nonverbal and are considered gestures by linguists.

Gestures add enormously to the richness of human expression. They can emphasize meaning, amplify it or even reverse it. One expert, Ray L. Birdwhistell of the University of Pennsylvania, believes that the face alone is capable of making 250,000 different combinations of gestures, and he classifies those commonly used by Americans into some 32 basic expressions.

The influence of this often-ignored form of communication is astonishingly pervasive. It establishes personal relationships, helps determine who is to be trusted and who is not, and even plays surprising roles in activities that are seemingly unrelated to language. Schoolteachers, for example, often signal by gestures their expectations of success or failure from students—and unconsciously encourage them to great-er achievement or, conversely, may discourage them so much that their abilities are never developed.

The gestural positioning of voice and body that says so much is in-deed a language, a creation of the people who use it. Within each cultural group the gestures are the same for all people and are, within that group, universally understood. Certain individuals may gesture more often and more broadly than others, just as some people speak more loudly and emphatically than their nelghbors. Some American men frequently and jovially slap their friends (and even comparative strangers) on the back, while others would never touch their closest friends except to shake hands. But all Americans understand what a friendly slap on the back means; they know that it is not an attack and that the backslapper's intentions are benign.

Beyond the cultural group, unspoken language displays the regional and social differences La Guardia demonstrated so well. Most West-erners shake the head from side to side to indicate "no" and bob the head up and down to signal "yes." But in Naples the custom is dif-ferent: "no" is indicated by jerking the head upward while sticking out the lower lip. Westerners glower with knitted eyebrows and sharp looks to suggest anger while other people abruptly raise the entire head, keep-ing the facial expression bland. People of various nations and regions differ in the amount of gesturing they do. The English, as might be ex-pected, are restrained, not to say stiff. In America, the immobile faces of the Down-East Yankees of the Northeastern Seaboard contrast with the greater expressiveness of Middle Westerners. In like fashion, var-ious people show differences in the way they stand, in their proximity to one another when they speak, in the frequency with which they touch one another. All these varieties of nonverbal signal tell a good deal about the world's cultures, about how people around the globe behave and interact, and about what their attitudes and assumptions are. How people gesture, in short, tells almost as much about how they commu-nicate as does the language they speak.

The human ability to communicate through gesture is surely ancient. Before early man invented language he presumably communicated pri-marily through gesture—pointing toward game, grimacing to show anger, perhaps laughing to show delight. It has long been debated wheth-er the signs that people use today have been inherited from the primitive signs employed by man's predecessors. Is the rictus of laughter, for ex-ample—the drawing back of the lips, the showing of teeth and the opening of the mouth—an expression man has inherited from past ages

The flirtatious glossary of the fan

Coyly manipulating her fan, the young woman at left signals "I love you" to a secret suitor. By the late 19th Century, when she was photographed, the fan had evolved from its origins as a cooling aid and fly chaser to a fashion accessory and, finally, to a device with which to send complex messages. In Spain, France, England and the United States, codes of fan language developed. One of them, used in Europe and America, appears below.

Carrying in left hand ...
          DESIROUS OF ACQUAINTANCE.

Placing it on left ear ...
          YOU HAVE CHANGED.

Twirling in left hand ...
          I WISH TO GET RID OF YOU.

Drawing across forehead ...
          WE ARE WATCHED.

Carrying in right hand ...
          YOU ARE TOO WILLING.

Drawing across the cheek ...... I LOVE YOU.

Drawing through the hand ..... I HATE YOU.

Drawing across the eyes .... I AM SORRY.

Letting it rest on right cheek .... YES.

Letting it rest on left cheek .... NO.

With handle to lips .... KISS ME.

Dropping .... WE WILL BE FRIENDS.

Closing it .... I WISH TO SPEAK TO YOU.

Open and shut .... YOU ARE CRUEL.

Open wide .... WAIT FOR ME.

so that it has become innate? Or does each generation of children have to learn to laugh by watching their parents? The fact that some human gestures, like laughter, are identical all over the world suggests they may be innate.

It has even been proposed, most notably by the great naturalist Charles Darwin, that man may have inherited some of his gestures from the apes. It is incontrovertible that chimpanzees bare their teeth in something that looks much like human laughter. But they also bare their teeth in anger. Whatever the value of Darwin's idea, there is no doubt that animals communicate gesturally with their kind. Certain male birds perform elaborate mating dances to advertise their eagerness and availability to females. Such dances bear some resemblance to human courtship gestures. In fact, there are a number of intriguing parallels between animal behavior and human gesture. It is suggestive that the human bow of peaceful and friendly greeting exposes a vulnerable spot, the back of the neck. The deep bow of fealty once accorded monarchs seems almost certainly to have symbolized, "Here, my Lord, is my neck; cut off my head if that is your pleasure." The same sort of message is conveyed by a dog when it rolls over on its back, exposing its throat and belly, its two most vulnerable spots. But whether any such parallels indicate a genuine evolutionary link is most uncertain.

While the origins of nonverbal language are murky, the reasons for its survival among glib-tongued modern men are not. Many gestures are more quickly comprehended than speech, and some are understandable around the world, transcending all the differences that may exist in the spoken language; thus gestures are preferred in moments of stress, when instant and unmistakable communication is essential. Because such signals are transmitted visually, they can travel much farther than spoken words, and they are unaffected by the presence of noise that would drown out speech. The referee at a boxing match would find it impossible to make his voice heard above the roar of the crowd and so he takes the winner s hand and holds it aloft to signal the fighter's triumph. Similarly, a pilot in a roaring jet fighter makes a circle of his thumb and first finger before take-off, the okay sign used to indicate that everything is functioning properly.

Such finger and arm signs have become distinctive elements in almost all activities and they resemble the technical jargon of a trade or sport. A thumb jerk meant life or death to a defeated gladiator in ancient Rome; today among stevedores it means that a load is ready to be hoisted. A recording engineer in his booth cannot verbally interrupt a musician by saying that time is up; he signals "cut" by drawing a finger across his throat. A broad repertoire of similar signs is used by police officers directing traffic, tennis umpires, the landing signal officer who guides pilots to landings on an aircraft carrier and by technicians in every field.

Other substitutes for words serve less serious—but perhaps no less important—ends. When an Arab sees a pretty girl he can silently communicate his approval by stroking his beard if he has one, his chin if he does not. According to Ray Birdwhistell, Italians make the same wordless comment by pulling on the lobe of one ear. Americans sometimes communicate that message by moving both hands to outline the curvaceous shape of a full-blown beauty. These gestures are not necessary; the Italian could murmer, "Bellissima," or the American, "Wow!" The gestures are made either because they are entertaining or because they are brief and emphatic.

These kinds of gestures, all of which take the place of words, are technically called emblems. They are relatively easy to understand—and indeed, would be useless if unclear. Other types of gestures accompany speech, rather than substituting for it, to regulate what is being said, or demonstrate it, or amplify it or comment upon it. A fisherman holds his hands apart to illustrate what he is saying about the fish that got away, and a wife describing an antique table she wants to buy will use her arms to show her husband how wide it is. Everybody points when giving a stranger directions.

While the emblems that replace words are generally hand or arm signals, the other types of gestures can be made in a variety of ways. Almost any sign from the flicker of an eyelid to a change in voice pitch can influence the meaning of what is said. The hands, however, provide the most obvious supplement to speech. Everyone uses them, consciously or unconsciously, at least occasionally while talking.

One simple hand gesture that is employed by many people is a cutting motion. If a man says that the company has cut off his pet project in order to save money on overhead costs, he will probably—and without having to think about it—chop downward with one hand to illustrate and emphasize the verb "cut." A few hand gestures that the reader may recognize as movements he himself uses include the hand held level, palm down, to accompany any statement meaning "I'm going to level with you"; the hands held out in front of the torso with the fingers spread in the shape of a bowl, to mean something like "That's all of it"; the opening of one palm and then the other to mean "on the one hand, and then on the other." Some of these hand and arm gestures seem to be universal, but the manner in which they are executed varies from culture to culture. While an American or Englishman makes a bowl with his hands to indicate "That's all of it," an Italian will characteristically throw his arms wide to make a more dramatic, more inclusive gesture meaning "all."

The Frenchman conveys a somewhat similar idea with a completely different gesture. To indicate "That's all there is" in the sense of an empty larder that is the result of economic reversal, he makes a belt-tightening sign, drawing his hand palm-up across his waist. The French put their own twist to other signals as well. Flicking the thumb and fingers together—a symbol that is widely used to convey talkativeness in the United States—means "shut up" in France. But Gallic gestures are peculiarly Gallic; only in France does pulling on the lower eyelid signal disbelief or rubbing the knuckles along the chin while looking upward mean boredom.

Similar variations can be seen among individuals within any culture, and most people have characteristic gestures of their own. The late President John F. Kennedy frequently employed an idiosyncratic forearm stab to emphasize what he was saying. American social commentator Will Rogers is remembered for pulling his forelock to indicate bemused puzzlement when finishing a joke that poked fun at some social foible.

Former French President Charles de Gaulle habitually accompanied his measured speech with slow, even ponderous, arm gestures that seemed to imply he could enclose all of France in his large embrace. The Soviet Union's ebullient Premier Nikita Khrushchev employed abrupt stabbing motions and, on one famous occasion at the United Nations, enlivened the history of political gesture by taking off his shoe and banging it on his desk.

If the hands talk forcefully, the face speaks more gently but more eloquently. The slight arching of an eyebrow, the curl of a lip, the almost imperceptible wrinkling of the skin around the eyes—these small signs are a continuous obbligato to all conversation. The fact that people normally change expression constantly while they are speaking—or as they encounter the vicissitudes of everyday life—was demonstrated in an unusual way by the great comedian of silent films, Buster Keaton. The

In cattle markets wherever Norsemen once roamed, in Normandy, England and Scandinavia, hand-slapping is the signal —audible, visible and physical—that seals the deal. This enduring custom typifies man's need to reinforce verbal agreements with bodily contact.

very core of Keaton's comedy was his rigid expression. It never changed. No matter what perils befell him, Keaton refused to smile or frown and instead maintained a perfectly immobile visage. This stone face struck the audiences watching Keaton's performances as being so odd, so bizarre, so completely contrary to normal human behavior, that they howled with laughter.

Some facial gestures are obvious. Even a little five-year-old girl will make an unmistakable display of courtship when in a boy's presence. She hides her mouth with her hands as if in embarrassment, looks down and away—and then looks back toward the boy with coquettish "follow me" glances. These gestures are found among children—and adults—in places as different as Norway and Central Africa, Saskatchewan and Thailand; they appear to be worldwide as well as obvious.

Many other facial gestures are so subtle and so transient that they cannot be easily observed by the naked eye and can be detected only by taking slow-motion movies of people talking. The films reveal faint but extremely precise motions—flickerings of cheek muscles, minute twitchings of the lips and tiny eyebrow movements—proof of the delicacy with which the brain controls the many muscles and nerves that are concentrated in the face. It appears that a child not only learns the exquisite controls of the facial muscles that make talking possible but also picks up the finely tuned coordination of the other facial muscles that control expression.

The plainest facial expression is the smile. Oddly, it also turns out to be one of the most ambiguous. A smile, it would seem, ought to be the same the world over—a universal and automatic reaction to the feeling of pleasure. But some people smile far more often than others and under different circumstances, depending on their personality and their culture. Ray L. Birdwhistell noted that smiling faces are far more frequently seen in the American Midwest and in the Southern cities of Atlanta, Louisville, Memphis and Nashville than in New England or upstate New York. It is perfectly appropriate for a young girl to saunter down Peachtree Street in Atlanta with a smile on her face. However, such behavior would seem distinctly odd to the more dour passersby on Main Street in Buffalo. As Birdwhistell says, "In one part of the country, an unsmiling individual might be queried as to whether he was 'angry about something,' while in another, the smiling individual might be asked, 'What's funny?' "

In addition, the smile does not always indicate happiness or pleasure. Some people smile when in doubt or when stoically accepting a piece of bad news. In some societies a smile can mean embarrassment while in others it can indicate that the smiling individual is under severe tension and may soon show hostility.

After the mouth, with its smile, the most expressive part of the face is the eyes. As the poet Henry Wadsworth Longfellow once put it, "He speaketh not; and yet there lies/A conversation in his eyes." Movements of the eyes, brows and lids indicate anger, joy, sorrow, love, questioning, sympathy. More important, a direct interaction between the eyes of two people—eye contact, it is called—is a major channel of communication between them and provides an essential indicator of their relationship to each other.

Psychologist Albert Mehrabian found that if a man rather dislikes the person to whom he is talking, he avoids eye contact as much as he possibly can. Women react differently. When women talk to other women whom they dislike, they maintain far more eye contact then men do in exactly the same circumstance—possibly lending some support to the idea that women are more skillful than men are at establishing and preserving smooth and pleasant social relationships. Eye contact approaches a maximum for both sexes, Mehrabian reported, not when a person feels friendly toward the other, but rather when his feelings about the other are neutral.

What the eyes say when the mutual feeling is very, very friendly indeed is a matter of some dispute. Mehrabian believes that eye contact lessens between lovers, reinforcing the notion nourished by generations of romantic novelists: An attraction between the sexes is marked by shy, downcast glances. But on this point, Mehrabian and the romantics are contradicted by Harvard psychologist Zick Rubin, who found that lovers look at each other a great deal.

The warmth of a loving glance and smile is not easily missed, but some gestures do not seem to be gestures at all, and their importance as part of unspoken language is often completely overlooked. Perhaps the most unusual and unexpected of these subtle signals is space: the physical distance between people. In Western society it clearly identifies the nature of their relationship to one another. But the distance between people also varies markedly from country to country in the West and even more between Western cultures and those of Asia and Africa. A leading student of spatial meaning, Edward T. Hall, wrote: "Spatial changes give a tone to a communication, accent it, and at times even override the spoken word. The flow and shift of distance between people as they interact with each other is part and parcel of the communication process."

Hall pinpointed the normal conversational distance between white Americans at 21 inches—almost two feet and almost at arm's length. Positioned closer than that, Americans generally feel uncomfortable. Situated much farther away from one another, they feel that the space is too great for the normal conversational topics and the normal conversational tone of voice. But people of many other cultures, including Arabs, Latin Americans and southern Europeans, are accustomed to standing much closer when they talk. When a person from one of these cultures talks to an American, the result can be ludicrous and even disturbing. "If a person gets too close," Hall noted, "the reaction is instantaneous and automatic—the other person backs up. . . . I have observed an American backing up the entire length of a long corridor while a foreigner whom he considers pushy tries to catch up with him. This scene has been enacted thousands and thousands of times—one per-

Most people need no words to tell what is under a barber pole (top, far right), but only Western Europeans are familiar with signs

for billiard parlor (top, far left), stained-glass maker (top left, center), wine shop (bottom, far left), and builder (top right, center).

son trying to increase the distance in order to be at ease, while the other tries to decrease it for the same reason."

Hall set up four categories for the various spaces in which communication can take place in America *(pages 81-83)*. There is, first of all, "intimate" distance, which ranges from the embrace of lovers out to 18 inches. (It is the foreigner's invasion of this 18-inch barrier, the intrusion into intimate space, that so disturbs Americans.) Hall's next category is "personal" distance—18 inches to four feet. This separation is suitable for conversation, at least among the white North Americans whom Hall studied. The next distance category Hall named "social" distance. At this point—four to 12 feet—intimate conversation is impossible. The four-foot inner limit, however, is appropriate for the impersonal chatter that typically occurs at a cocktail party, while the outer limit is suitable for a boss who is giving instructions to his secretary. Beyond the 12-foot limit there is "public" distance. At such long range all informal communication becomes impossible; the speaker does not converse, he gives a speech, choosing his words carefully and changing to a "public" tone of voice.

Dramatic examples of the way in which distance can be manipulated for special purposes are afforded by the military. A Marine drill sergeant will chew out a recruit by yelling at him while they are standing almost nose to nose. The sergeant blatantly and insultingly invades the rookie's intimate space. On the other hand, when an enlisted man presents himself to an officer he is kept at a distance. The officer is usually behind a desk and the man reporting is expected to stop and salute well on the far side of it. Thus the customs prescribed by the military prevent any intimacy between officers and men, or between higher and lower ranking officers, when they are on official business. The transaction remains wholly formal—and impersonal.

Arabs' sense of space, according to Edward T. Hall, is almost totally different from that of Europeans or Americans. Arabs do not mind being crowded by other people; they are used to having to push and shove and having bodily contact with others in a jam-packed bazaar. But they detest the feeling of being crowded or hemmed in by walls. They want their rooms to be large and uncluttered, with very high ceilings. In conversation the Arabs enjoy being close, so close in fact that the other person's breath and body odor can easily be smelled. Or they can be comfortable conversing at considerable distances. An Arab can sit in a chair that is fully 40 feet away from his listener and not feel uncomfortably distant. People of Western cultures intensely dislike being breathed on—they need far more distance to be comfortable. Likewise,

continued on page 84

Forced into "intimate" proximity—18 inches or less—passengers on a New York ferry turn from one another for a feeling of distance.

The meaning of distance

The commuters in the jammed ferryboat above are expressing a paradox, wordlessly. The crowding requires them to sit close, and the nearness has a meaning—it is a spacing reserved for intimacy. But these people are strangers. Each reacts to this invasion of intimate territory by contradicting the spacing statement with posture and expression: His neighbors are not intimates and do not belong so close.

The language of social space, which was named proxemics by one of its pioneer investigators, anthropologist Edward T. Hall, varies from culture to culture. Arabs indicate polite friendliness by a close distance, which to Americans, Englishmen and Germans means loving or comforting attention.

In Hall's view social distance expresses what is acceptable or intrusive in different circumstances. He found four categories of separation from intimate closeness to the "public" distance between speaker and audience. Hall measured the categories *(above and overleaf)* by observing a limited group —middle-class people in the Northeastern United States—but his findings seem to apply to most Americans.

A "personal" distance of 18 inches up to four feet is appropriate for college friends at dance practice.

Anthropology students conferring with their teacher defer to his status by keeping a respectful distance, four to 12 feet. Such "social" spacings are common among people who work together.

Standing on a platform high above the crowd, activist Bobby Seale delivers a speech against the Vietnam War in San Francisco in 1972. His position follows the "public" distance rule: 12 feet or more between speaker and audience.

they feel that conversation is impossible across a distance of 40 feet. The Arabs, for their part, cannot comprehend the intermediate distances preferred by Westerners. A Westerner conversing from what he considers a normal conversational distance—say two or three feet —seems to the Arab to be cold, aloof, even hostile. Such misunderstandings, according to observers of Middle Eastern politics, have more than once soured European and American diplomatic moves in that part of the world.

The ultimate extension of spacing is bodily contact; at that point it becomes a gesture that can hardly be missed and seldom misinterpreted. And just as the people of some societies and ethnic groups stand closer to one another when they converse—or even simply when they stand in a crowd or in a line outside a movie house—so some peoples are far more likely to touch one another during discourse. Some peoples enjoy bodily contact while others avoid it except in the most intimate circumstances. It has often been observed that the British and the French, although their nations are separated by only 21 miles across the English Channel, could hardly be more different in this regard. Frenchmen are likely to greet their male friends by kissing them on both cheeks; Englishmen, for whom bodily contact in public is taboo, often avoid even a handshake. French parents frequently and openly express their affection for their children; an Englishman (at least of the old school) may peck his daughters on the cheek but keeps a rigidly formal distance from his sons.

That such characteristics, though stereotypes, have a basis in fact is indicated by the studies of psychologist S. M. Jourard. He found contrasts between the behavior of couples seated in cafés in various parts of the world. In a café in San Juan, Puerto Rico, he observed that the men and women who were seated as couples touched each other an average of 180 times per hour. In Paris the couples touched 110 times an hour. In a city in Florida, where the majority of the customers of the café were white and middle-class, the couples touched on the average of twice an hour. In London the couples that Jourard observed managed somehow not to touch each other at all.

There is one kind of gesture that only a linguist would describe as a gesture. It is vocal but it is not verbal: paralanguage, the changes in tone of voice and emphasis that a speaker gives to the words he is uttering. It is classified as gesturing by scholars because tone and emphasis, like facial gestures, have a profound influence on the meaning of what is being said. In fact, how something is said is frequently more important than what is said.

The vocal cues that accompany the spoken words often contradict the apparent meaning of the words. In sarcasm, the intonation and tone of voice that are employed plainly supersede the surface meaning of the words. It is possible to say, "Oh, that's great!" in such a way that the sentence really means, "That's awful." Someone who has just returned from a vacation on which he spent two rainy weeks at a supposedly sunny resort at the seashore might say, "We had a wonderful time," in such a way his listener would perceive instantly that the message he intended to convey was just the opposite.

But paralanguage can achieve effects more subtle than the outright reversal of sarcasm. Such a plain, brief sentence as "He's a pleasant man" can mean half a dozen different things depending on the manner in which it is spoken. Spoken slowly with emphasis given to both of the last two words—"He's a (pause) pleasant (pause) man"—it has a tone of complete sincerity; the speaker obviously believes that the person under discussion is indeed a genial, honest and trustworthy fellow. But spoken more quickly with the voice falling off to a flat monotone on the last two words—"He's a (brief pause) pleasant man"—the sentence

A Marine drill instructor lets a recruit know who is boss at Parris Island, South Carolina, with a stare more expressive than any words. Such aggressive eye contact can be traced, according to some experts, back through evolution to primate behavior: It is related to the aggressiveness of an ape that is staring down an intruder in its territory.

means something entirely different. This individual is blameless enough, in the speaker's opinion—there is nothing really wrong with him—but there is nothing about him to inspire any great enthusiasm either. In between these two extremes would be a quickly spoken "He's-a-pleasant-man," with the voice holding a steady, cheerful, rising tone. Translated this might mean something like, "He's quite friendly and much like the general run of decent people."

George L. Trager, a pioneer in the study of vocal cues, identified dozens of such gestures that people make with their voices. They can vary their tonal pitch, of course, or maintain a monotone. They can speak forcefully, with strong emphasis, or in a relaxed and lazy manner. Their speech rhythms can be fast or slow, smooth or jerky. They can make their voices more or less resonant. They can yell the words they speak or whisper them, can moan or groan or whine. Sighing out words can imply boredom or hopelessness (or perhaps mock despair). A slow and stately delivery implies that the speaker has given the matter careful thought and is handing down a definitive judgment. Everybody is aware that actors skillfully utilize this full arsenal of tricks in their performances. But the average person seldom reflects that he, too, employs such vocal cues—not all of them, perhaps, but those that have become habitual—every day. In fact, he could not speak without employing some of them for, like facial and bodily gestures, they are the invariable concomitant of speech.

Beyond the direct usefulness of paralanguage in communicating meaning is a secondary but strangely important role for this type of gesture. It is often the basis by which an individual's personal qualities are judged. Most people are conscious that they are prejudiced against some paralinguistic styles; nobody likes a child who whines as he talks. But not everybody in Western cultures is aware of the existence of a widespread prejudice in favor of a man who has a low, deep voice, especially a man who speaks slowly and yet manages to avoid pomposity. Somehow people trust those who are gifted with—or who have carefully cultivated—low, resonant tones. It would be difficult to think of a television newscaster with a high, squeaky voice, or of a popular dramatic actor. Comedians can succeed even if they have high-pitched voices, but for heroes it helps immeasurably to sound like Richard Burton or Jean Gabin. A low-toned huskiness does not seem to do any harm to the careers of actresses either—think of Lauren Bacall and Marlene Dietrich.

How far the influence of the deep voice extends is a matter of argument. Some trusted national leaders, such as Winston Churchill and Charles de Gaulle, have possessed reassuringly deliberate and low-

pitched voices. Others attained equal power despite rather high-pitched vocal tones: Franklin D. Roosevelt, Dwight D. Eisenhower and, in particular, Theodore Roosevelt.

The question has long intrigued psychologists, who have run repeated tests to see whether vocal cues are in fact reliable guides to personality. They have played recordings of various voices to test subjects and asked the subjects to rate the voices. Did they think the voices indicated leadership qualities or extroversion, sociability, intelligence? The psychologists then gave the people whose voices they had recorded standard personality tests in order to determine whether the characteristics that had been observed in their voices would show up in the tests. The results so far have been what scientists gently call "inconclusive"—they prove nothing.

All of the ways in which people supplement words—tone, eye contact, smiles, hand and arm signals, personal spacing—may be examined separately, but in day-to-day communication they are likely to be used together. A sequence of gestures gets underway even before any conversation starts, according to psychiatrist Albert Scheflen. When friends approach each other on the street or meet face to face at a party, Scheflen said, they almost invariably display a three-stage ritual of recognition. First the head jerks upward slightly, then the eyelids rise, widening the eyes as a glance is exchanged, and finally the eyebrows shoot upward in the "eyebrow flash." The three gestures occur so swiftly that they seem almost simultaneous. Furthermore, Scheflen reported that this ritual of recognition is common in virtually every culture around the globe.

Curiously, a comparable ritual takes place when two strangers approach each other in an uncrowded space such as a largely deserted sidewalk or an open field. At a distance of about 15 feet, each will look up and glance at the other, silently acknowledging the other's presence. But then strangers will abruptly look down and away, avoiding any further eye contact.

Sociologist Erving Goffman of the University of Pennsylvania coined the phrase "civil inattention" to describe this curious process —"civil" because, while both strangers recognize that the other person exists, each refuses to invade the other's privacy. The ritual of civil inattention occurs in many cultures with slight variations. Among natives of the urban, eastern sections of North America the glance the two strangers flash each other is swift and fleeting; among Latin Americans the eye contact tends to last longer. To people who are accustomed to brief eye contact, a more lingering glance can be extremely disconcerting. "Does he think he knows me? Have I just snubbed someone I've been introduced to?" Such doubts assail the person who has just received a longer glance than he expected.

Eye contact is so important to recognition or lack of it because it signals whether or not the channel of communication is open. That is the reason strangers, as they approach each other, glance up very briefly but then immediately look away; to maintain eye contact would be to invite, almost to demand, further communication. Streetwalkers signal their availability in unmistakable fashion simply by staring at every passing male—their attempt to lengthen the eye contact is in itself an invitation.

In some circumstances eye contact almost obliges interaction. A person in a restaurant who wishes to order something tries to "catch the waiter's eye." His eye once caught, the waiter knows that the customer wants to open a channel of communication. As many frustrated customers have discovered, some waiters are positive geniuses at avoiding eye contact. Most people will also remember the problem of eye contact in the classroom. When the instructor asks a difficult question, most students immediately look down at their notes, or out the window, or into their desks—anywhere but at the teacher. The last thing any of these students wants is to have eye contact, to signal the instructor that the channel of communication is open. And everybody has tried desperately to avoid the bore at a party by looking away whenever the bore seemed to be edging closer.

Once eye contact has been established by the three-stage ritual of recognition described by Scheflen, both friends will raise a hand, usually palm outward, and will utter a verbal salutation such as "Hi, Bill." Then the two, if they want to talk, will approach each other with hands outstretched.

Showing the palm of the hand, as people do when they greet a friend at a distance, is apparently a deeply ingrained gesture that humans share with the anthropoid apes. The British zoologist Jane Goodall, who has observed chimpanzees in the wild more attentively than anyone else, reported that if a young chimp of low status in his chimpanzee troop or band wants to eat a banana when a senior chimp is nearby, the junior chimp presents its hand palm-up to the senior. The senior gives approval by patting this upturned palm with its own palm. Only then will the younger chimpanzee dare to go ahead and eat the fruit. A similar palm signal is employed by a female chimpanzee that has had a baby. When the infant chimp is old enough to be presented to the troop, the mother takes the baby and goes around to the troop's grown members with palm up as a gesture of entreaty. When the corresponding gesture of approval has been granted, the youngster is formally admitted into the band.

Whether man has inherited this open-palm gesture from his apelike ancestors is not known. It would be a natural gesture for man to have developed on his own as a way of inaugurating a peaceful conversation, for it clearly shows that he conceals nothing in his hand and is unarmed —it signals that he has no hostile intentions and wishes to be friends. Other common human gestures of friendship may also derive from signals that a man is forgoing armed hostility. Raising the hat in greeting, some experts believe, may derive from an ancient practice of doffing a military helmet, just as the salute may date back to the days when men raised their helmets' visors to say they came in peace.

Once negotiations for opening a conversation are completed, they are followed by ritualistic symbols and signals involved in keeping it going. These visual punctuation marks act like a policeman at an in-

tersection to impose order on the flow of conversational traffic. Without them people would constantly speak at once.

A leading investigator of the gestural punctuation marks that regulate conversational give-and-take is Starkey Duncan Jr. of the University of Chicago. Duncan found that a listener encourages the speaker to continue by humming a noncommittal "mmm," or by signaling agreement with a nod of the head or another tone, "uh huh." If he wants to interrupt he does not simply begin talking, even though he has plenty of opportunity—speakers pause so much they make sounds only 50 to 60 per cent of the time and the average vocalization lasts less than two seconds. Instead, if the listener in a two-person conversation wishes to break in and say something he will employ one or more of four standard gestures.

The most important interruption signal is a shift of the head; the man who wishes to start speaking looks away abruptly before he begins. Another cue is audible inhalation—the would-be speaker breathes in abruptly and loudly enough to be heard. The third cue is a gesticulation of the hands, either outthrust slightly or curled into a loose fist. The fourth cue is vocal tone: the person wishing to interrupt does so, but in a loud voice. This last paralinguistic cue is most often used when there has been some confusion about who is to speak—the other turn-taking cues either have not been given or have not been noticed—and both conversants speak at once. The one speaking more loudly generally prevails and takes the floor.

But what if the original speaker is not finished with what he has to say and does not wish to give way? Duncan found that in such cases the speaker uses two of the cues the would-be speaker employs: the abrupt shift of the head and the hand gesticulation. When a speaker uses these cues, especially the hand movements, he overrides any interruption cues displayed by the listener. "It was found," Duncan says, "that display of the gesticulation signal virtually eliminates claims to the turn by the auditor." This "speaker continuation signal" is understood unconsciously by all listeners and they play their part in this elaborate gestural game by keeping silent.

This entire elaborate minuet of gestural moves and countermoves takes place, it appears, whenever two speakers are having a lively, interested exchange. Other signals are used in addition if the conversation is not going well, when one of the conversants is bored or tired or dubious. One of the subtle signals of conversational distress, especially important because it is taken as a measure of the worth of what is said, is looking away, especially down.

Two Argentinian gauchos communicate their affection for each other with a hearty abrazo after a day on the town drinking, chatting and playing cards. Such body contact between males—a means of expressing friendship almost nonexistent in English-speaking countries—is common practice in many other cultures.

Matinee idol Rudolph Valentino pops his eyes to convey his passion for an overwhelmed Alla Nazimova in the 1921 picture Camille.

Showing passion in the silents

For three decades the movies got along without spoken dialogue, and the lack of sound did not interfere with the stories. The language of the silents was largely gesture, and it was understandable to fans in the farthest balconies.

To make sure nobody missed fine dramatic points, the players exaggerated all of their actions. Mugging, leering, glowering, glaring and scowling became stock expressions, and some actors went at it with such great enthusiasm that at crucial moments they looked as though they had been suddenly jabbed with a pin, or were in danger of swooning unless the smelling salts were brought quickly.

The graceful hand at the forehead means
Anna Q. Nilsson is distraught in
If I Marry Again: her husband was abandoning her.

The parson looks more than normally pious, the bride demure, while the
groom, Slim Summerville, ogles a pretty leg in a silent comedy.

Armed with an over-sized knife and scowling fiercely to
demonstrate sincerity, Mae Marsh threatens
to do herself in during Hoo Doo Ann. (She later changed her mind.)

This turn of the eyes is not the shy glance of courtship or the abrupt looking away of the listener about to interrupt but is more akin to the avoidance of eye contact indicating dislike. In most Western nations a polite listener looks the speaker in the eye much of the time he is speaking—not with a steady stare, but with an interested gaze. Refusing eye contact and looking away steadily indicates that the listener is bored —or is highly dubious about what is being said. And the listener will be made dubious if the speaker looks away.

A gaze that is straightforward and steady is assumed to be an indication of the individual's truthfulness. Most people in the Western world believe that a man who "looks you straight in the eye" when he talks should be taken at his word. Shifty-eyed people, by contrast, are assumed to be dishonest.

This belief in the testimony of eye contact, firmly embedded in Western culture, seems to be partly justified—but only partly. To test it, a group at the University of North Carolina was given a rigged test of group decision-making ability. Each subject took the test in company with another person, supposedly a second subject but actually a confederate of the psychologist conducting the experiment. Halfway through the test the psychologist who had been monitoring the two was called away by prearrangement to receive a telephone call. In his absence the confederate suggested to the subject that they look at the answer sheet. Most of the subjects were willing to give in to this suggestion and did cheat.

When the psychologist returned, he accused the subjects of cheating. Some of them confessed almost immediately. Among those who chose to lie and deny their guilt, some had difficulty looking the psychologist in the face. They became shifty-eyed, unable to sustain a direct gaze. Some of the cheaters, however, not only seemed able to look their accuser in the eye, but actually increased eye contact beyond the normal. They consciously used an exaggeratedly direct gaze to lend credence to their statements even while they brazenly lied. The gifted liars uncovered in this test were classed as "Machiavellians," after the great Italian political philosopher Niccolò Machiavelli, who counseled kings and princes that, to safely navigate the treacherous waters of statecraft, they must become adept at evading the truth.

It would seem that the man who could master eye movements and look convincingly sincere might be able to lie his way through life and never be discovered. But the perfect liar, if he exists at all, must be a very rare bird. There are other gestures besides eye movements that indicate truth or falsity in a conversation.

Paul Ekman and Wallace V. Friesen, among the most respected scientists studying gestural language, have observed the unconscious gestures through which people betray nervousness or an attempt at deception. The body, Ekman and Friesen said, is more likely to show this "leakage" than the eyes or face because people from childhood on are accustomed to controlling facial activity. Every child learns that when he has stolen a forbidden candy he had better keep a straight face in front of his mother. Children are admonished not to "make faces" in the presence of guests. All this training results, Ekman and Friesen reported, in "greater awareness of ongoing facial activity" and therefore a greater ability to lie with the face.

But the body receives no such training and attention. "The body . . . usually more truthfully reveals to the observer either how the person actually feels (leakage) or the fact that something is amiss," Ekman and Friesen found. They discovered that the face usually does reveal the fact that a person is hiding something or lying, but it does so in "microexpressions"—tiny movements so fleeting that they can be seen only in slow-motion film and are invisible to the ordinary observer. The control of the face is good enough to fool most people. But a fluttering of a hand, a swinging leg, a tapping foot, jerky movements of the body —these are the giveaways.

Long before these gestures of deceit were demonstrated by experiment, they were recognized for what they were by the greatest psychologist of all, Sigmund Freud. Freud knew that people can say more with their bodies than with words: "He that has eyes to see and ears to hear may convince himself that no mortal can keep a secret. If his lips are silent, he chatters with his finger tips; betrayal oozes out of him at every pore."

Actions louder than words

In a classic pantomime, the French performer Marcel Marceau attends an imaginary cocktail party and makes his way through a receiving line. He meets a beautiful girl and beams. Then he stifles a yawn while confronting a boring guest and listens to another tell a funny story. The mime brilliantly communicates all of these encounters—silently, on an empty stage—because he has mastered, and his audience recognizes, the eloquent repertoire of gestures, expressions and body movements that all speakers use to make their meaning clear. So essential are these actions that one expert, R. L. Birdwhistell, suggests that as much as 65 per cent of conversational exchanges may be nonverbal.

Nonverbal communication does vary from culture to culture. When an American stretches out his hand, with palm upward, and beckons with his fingers, it means, "Come here." An Italian employs the same gesture to say, "Goodbye." Facial expressions and gestures also vary by social class and conversational style.

Despite the cultural, class or individual variations, however, psychologists Paul Ekman and Wallace Friesen have distinguished five general categories of nonverbal communication. They are: *illustrators*, actions that help explain or amplify the meaning of what is being said; *emblems*, gestures with precise meanings that can replace speech; *affect displays*, facial expressions that convey inner feelings; *regulators*, techniques that are used to control the flow of conversational exchanges; and *adaptors*, habitual gestures that are clues to the speaker's emotional state. By this measure, the eloquent comment by the motorist at right is an illustrator.

Trapped in a traffic jam in Rome, a disgusted Italian motorist relies on a time-honored gesture to accent his outburst of anger. The tightly clenched fingers, pressed against the thumb, mean, "What do you want, imbecile?"

Amplifying with gestures

Some gestures, the ones called illustrators by Ekman and Friesen, are spontaneous adjuncts to speech. A fisherman spreads his hands to show the size of his prize; a traffic policeman points a finger to indicate directions to a motorist; a politician pounds a lectern to underscore the rhythm of his rhetoric.

Each of these nonverbal communications serves to accent, to amplify or to dramatize the spoken word—making the message clearer and, at the same time, commanding heightened attention from the listener. Most illustrators are used deliberately and are widely shared within cultural groups.

An American cheerleader's acrobatic leaps emphasize her exhortations for a victory.

At a Russian wedding feast, a toast maker's sweeping gesture dramatizes his tribute to and expression of good wishes for the couple.

In the arcane language of the stock exchange, this broker's gesture says he will buy or sell when a price changes fractionally to 7/8.

"Peace" and "Power" are the symbols used by Chicago demonstrators.

Hand signals
that replace speech

At times when speech is impossible
or is inappropriate—for example, between two underwater swimmers, in the
clamor of a stock exchange or when a
commando squad patrols enemy territory—communication is carried out by
the gestures called emblems by students
of nonverbal behavior.

These gestures have precise meanings
and are readily understood: for example, a military salute is a respectful way
of saying, "Good day, Sir." Emblems
are used by specific groups for specific purposes, though some are widely
shared within a culture.

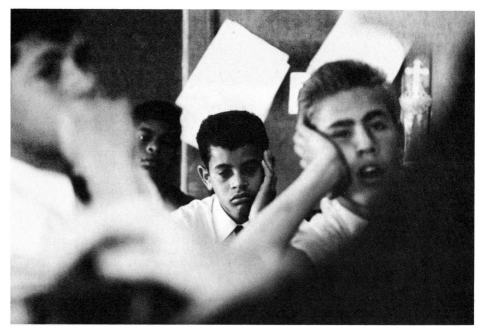

Slack expressions during a high school geography class express a shared feeling of boredom.

Feelings seen in the face

The face conveys so much information all by itself that in the opinion of some psychologists it ranks second only to speech as a means of communication. Facial expressions, known technically as affect displays, portray both pleasant and unpleasant feelings and also show the degree of intensity with which those feelings are held.

Scientists since Darwin have suggested that some facial displays, such as those that register anger, sadness or joy, are common to all mankind. Other experts argue that all affect displays are culturally learned. Whatever their origin may be, facial expressions are double-edged. They can reveal deep-felt emotions, and they also can be used for deception—for example, when a parent feigns anger to impress a reprimand upon a child.

Joy and disappointment are registered by the winner and loser at a teen-age beauty contest.

The pain-filled eyes of a village woman in Cyprus show her grief on learning of the death of her husband during civil strife in 1964.

Regulating a conversation, a Veronese man tells his comrade that he is listening by keeping close eye contact (above), then shows his impatience by scratching his head (center) and sits upright to take control of the conversation (bottom).

How to interrupt a conversation

The operator of a two-way radio signals that a transmission is ended by saying, "Over," thus letting his partner on the other end know that he may transmit. In normal conversation gestures or expressions often serve the same purpose and also regulate the pace of the exchange.

Steady eye contact or a nod of the head, for example, tell the speaker he is being listened to and should continue talking. When the listener looks away or drums his fingers impatiently, he is saying, in effect, "Stop talking," "Hurry up" or "Be more interesting." Although few speakers are fully aware of these regulators, the cues are common to all face-to-face communication.

A Roman arguing politics ignores his opponent's outstretched palm—a regulator intended to halt the tirade and permit a rejoinder.

Movements that betray the emotions

Habits picked up in childhood, such as pulling at a lock of hair or picking at the face, very often become a part of an individual's style of communication. These gestures and involuntary movements unconsciously reveal a person's inner states of anxiety, tension or discomfort. Psychologists call these non-verbal acts adaptors, and they usually involve touching some part of the body with the hands.

Although many adaptors are unique to a particular individual, some are widely used and easily interpreted. For example, when a speaker covers his eyes with his hands, it may indicate that he is trying to conceal or to avoid something that he finds unpleasant. Or when he twirls a pencil or bends paper clips, he may be making an attempt to control his nervousness.

107

Announcing an Identity

4

Whether he is a national leader like Walter Scheel *(left)*, surrounded by microphones as he holds a press conference in West Germany, or just an ordinary citizen in an everyday conversation, no one can speak without broadcasting his origins, his role in life, and ultimately his identity. For the language that every individual uses is the product of all the social forces that affect his behavior: the society in which he lives, his class, his occupation and his own unique experience.

The most basic influence on the individual's speech is the simple circumstance of the language that is spoken in the country of his birth. Its effect is much deeper than merely determining whether he says "auf Wiedersehen," "au revoir" or "goodbye." For the language systems that nations use are not just haphazard collections of speech sounds put together in arbitrary fashion. Every national language is a product of a special culture, and all the individuals who use it are influenced to think and behave in accordance with that culture's values.

Japan provides a clear example of the interaction between the national language and behavior. The Japanese are a stylized and highly stratified people whose conduct is carefully prescribed for almost every occasion, and the forms and proprieties of behavior are enshrined in their language. This sense of propriety can be seen in the way the Japanese use the first person singular pronoun. The Japanese language has some 45 different words meaning "I." Some are dialect words spoken only in certain parts of the country, but Standard Japanese, the language taught in the schools and used on radio and television, recognizes more than a dozen forms. They range from "chin," uttered only by the emperor on formal occasions, to "atai," used by little girls. "Boku" and "ore" are spoken only by males, the former used only when talking informally to close friends of the same age and status and the latter when speaking to inferiors. "Wa-re" is also for males, but it is the word a military or political leader would use when exhorting his followers. Refined females call themselves "watashi," and women of lower status say "atashi." "Watak'shi" is the safe word for "I" that foreigners learn and that all educated Japanese employ in polite situations.

No Japanese individual uses all the "I" pronouns, but every Japanese commands a repertoire of three or more of them and switches automatically from one to another as the conventions dictate. Every Japanese understands even those words for "I" that he does not use, and he would be quick to notice an inappropriate pronoun. Furthermore each of these pronouns normally accompanies a prescribed style of gesture, posture and bows that would seem out of place if a different pronoun were uttered; a Japanese male saying "boku," for example, may slouch, talk loudly and argue vigorously, but if a man refers to himself as "watak'shi" the chances are he is sitting or standing erectly and politely masking or at least softening his opinions.

The variety of words for the pronoun "I" is not a meaningless quirk of the Japanese language; rather, it is a crucial thread in the Japanese social fabric. The multiple forms reflect—and strengthen—the keen Japanese awareness that every individual has a particular niche and rank in the social order. The notion of human equality has had little importance in traditional Japanese society and the individual's rights and duties depend on who that individual is. A Japanese always thinks of himself in terms of his place and rank, and the choice of pronoun makes this both necessary and easy. Every time a Japanese says "I" he is reminded, if only subconsciously, that he is not just a human being but a particular kind of human being in a particular situation. In selecting the right word for "I," he is forced to pin a label on himself and to acknowledge his place in society. And by making that choice, and making it properly, he is certifying that he is Japanese.

I ndividual speech patterns, in Japan and elsewhere, are influenced by five major forces in addition to native tongue. The first and most noticeable influence on speech behavior after national language itself, is the region and particular locale in which the individual grows up. Regional dialects may be considered just as proper as a standard language, or they may be looked down upon as backward and inelegant. In any case, they do clearly reveal an individual's geographic origin.

Social class is another influential circumstance. Besides belonging to a country and a region, every individual, whether he likes it or not, is a member of some social class, and his accent, his grammar and his vocabulary tell the world which one—as Henry Higgins proved with Eliza Doolittle in George Bernard Shaw's *Pygmalion*. Some class variations are barely noticeable except to the trained ear; others, like the ghetto speech of black American children, are so distinctively structured they are regarded by some linguists as languages of their own.

A still narrower and more particular determinant of speech is group membership. Professions, occupations, criminal gangs, social cliques, sportsmen, political movements—all use specialized vocabularies and speech habits, and are identifiable by their own jargon, argot or slang.

Society's fourth important influence on an individual's use of language is the relationship that exists between speaker and listener. Older people and work superiors are addressed with respect; close friends are treated more casually. Language behavior, in other words, is affected by both status and intimacy.

Finally, every individual, every day, passes through a variety of speech situations, changing his vocabulary, his tone of voice and his grammar for each one, choosing topics and locutions that his total experience tells him are proper for that particular occasion. For example, the same idea may be expressed totally differently. A person indicating puzzlement at a public meeting might say, "I'd like to request further clarification of your last point." To his friends, he would say, "I may be dumb but I don't understand exactly what you're talking about," and at home the same idea becomes simply: "I don't get it."

Regional speech differences, the first of these categories, are primarily matters of pronunciation. Geographically compact nations with a more or less official standard pronunciation, like Britain, Japan, Germany and France, look down on regional dialects as inferior lingoes. To British speakers of Received Pronunciation, or RP (also known as BBC English), the regional accents of Britain carry many emotional overtones, and people who speak them have to endure the jibes and the prejudice of their compatriots.

Since the time of Chaucer, the stereotype of Northern English has been unflattering to its speakers. The harsh, rugged Northern speech "still presents itself to many southerners," says British linguist Walter Nash, indulging in some North Country dialect himself, "as a means of communication fit only for money-grubbing millowners, fiercely forthright matrons and gradely (if mildly moronic) lads." (In Yorkshire "gradely" means "upstanding" and "worthy.") Yorkshiremen and other northerners are expected to converse on business, commerce or manufacturing, but Nash finds it difficult to imagine a lecture on art or music delivered in North Country dialect. An entirely different picture is suggested to speakers of RP by the southwest dialect, the dialect of Thomas Hardy. The speech of the southwest suggests cricket commentators, gardeners, rosy-cheeked farmers and other tolerant, amiable and unhurried individuals, according to Nash, "but it has not escaped ridicule as the dialect of hayseeds and slow-grinding rustic wits."

The British prejudice against regional dialects is so strong that virtually no top corporation executive in London speaks with a local accent —even though many company officials come from the provinces. Some big companies secretly send rising young executives to expensive speech schools that specialize in erasing dialects, a long, difficult process.

Germany is another country where regional accents automatically conjure up stereotypes. The guttural, masculine Bavarian dialect, for instance, suggests to other Germans a noisy peasant babbling against the din of a brass band in a beer hall, but somehow the same dialect sounds capricious and appealing when spoken by young women. On the other hand, Saxonian, spoken in the neighboring province, seems petulant to most Bavarians; they say the Saxonians sound as if they are still carrying a chip on their shoulder because Charlemagne murdered thousands of their ancestors more than a millennium ago.

In a large country like the United States, regional accents are numerous and easily recognized—the Southern drawl, the New England twang and the flat tones of the Middle West. Perhaps the most distinctive are the so-called Brooklyn accent ("Moider duh bums"), which persists in the movies but is less often heard on the streets of Brooklyn, and the Elizabethan speech of the Appalachian mountain region ("I durst not do it" and "He'll be there against I get home"), which the rest of the country hears as issuing from the mouths of feuding moonshiners.

Pronunciation aside, an American's geographic origins are clearly revealed by a number of regional lexical quirks. New Yorkers, for instance, echoing the Dutch of New Amsterdam, say "stoop" for outside front steps; and they stand "on line" on the "sidewalk" while other city dwellers stand "in line" on the "pavement." Ozark housewives "red up" the table after a meal and Southerners say they are "real well" or "mighty fine." A Bostonian who orders a "frappe" would get blank looks south of Providence; his drink is a "milk shake" in Connecticut, New York and Philadelphia. Moving from New England to the Midwest, "sack" and "bag" change sizes: a sack of potatoes becomes a bag of potatoes, and a small paper bag becomes a small paper sack.

Regional dialects diverge for a number of reasons—sometimes because their speakers subconsciously want them to. In recent years the native residents of the summer resort island of Martha's Vineyard, off the coast of Massachusetts, have been gradually—and unconsciously—changing their pronunciation of several vowel sounds: "Right" now sounds almost like "ruyt," and "cow" and "house" have changed to something like "kew" and "hewse." This alteration puzzled linguists when it was first noticed because it seemed to defy the general trend in the country. The Vineyard pronunciations are regarded as plainer, less sophisticated sounds than the ones heard 30 years ago, although shifts in pronunciation generally reflect a popular desire to sound more elegant. The mystery was cleared up by a study by William Labov of the University of Pennsylvania that coupled linguistic research with a careful examination of the social attitudes of native Vineyarders.

This study revealed that the Vineyarders are unaware of the change but the residents whose speech displays the new pronunciations most clearly are those who are determined to remain on the island, in spite of the fact that economic opportunities there are few. They are the people who resent most keenly their social and economic domination by summer visitors from the mainland. By subconsciously reverting to an earlier pronunciation, by sounding their vowels in a way that differs distinctly from mainland speech, the oldtimers of Martha's

Before going on the air, broadcasters in India assume yoga-like postures as they compare the contents of their news scripts—each written in a different language. Around 200 languages are spoken in India. As a compromise with this linguistic diversity, the government network, All-India Radio, broadcasts in the 15 officially recognized tongues.

The handwritings on the walls

For as long as language has been written, people have been scrawling names, slogans and epithets on any blank surfaces they could find, proclaiming their identities and expressing their emotions to an audience they might never see. Egyptian workmen left their names on the walls of turquoise mines in the Sinai as early as 2500 B.C. In the First Century A.D., the people of Pompeii in Italy scrawled ads for gladiator contests on buildings. And sometimes they let loose invective: "May you be nailed to the cross," wrote a disgruntled patron of the public baths.

Because graffiti writing is often a solitary occupation, many graffiti are found in places occupied by one person at a time: public toilets, library study cubicles or prison cells.

Probably the most ubiquitous modern graffito is the American GI's boast, "Kilroy was here." Originated in World War II, it appears on the Statue of Liberty, under Paris' Arc de Triomphe and on China's Marco Polo Bridge.

A passerby studies Stockholm's official graffiti wall. It is regularly whitewashed to ready it for more free speech—a practice frowned on by graffiti admirers, who object to obliterating sentiments worth preserving for the sake of posterity.

Caught in the act—a rarity for graffiti artists—two boys chalk on a Belfast wall the political message "Remember 1690." It refers to the Battle of the Boyne, in which the Protestant forces defeated the Roman Catholics.

The anonymous city kid's desire for self-assertion is reflected in the graffiti blitz adorning this New York City subway train. The youngsters use spray cans of paint to write nicknames and the numbers of the streets where they live. The practice is illegal, but authorities have had very little success in curbing it.

Vineyard are asserting their local pride and distinguishing themselves from the summer people. Concluded Labov, "When a man says 'ruyt' or 'hewse,' he is unconsciously establishing the fact that he belongs on the island: that he is one of the natives to whom the island really belongs."

Just as each individual carries on his tongue the brand of his region of origin (unless he has had a strong enough motive to go to the great trouble and expense of eradicating it), he also exhibits the speech habits of a particular social class. This is the second major influence on the individual's speech.

Class distinctions may be confined to a region or may cut across all geographical boundaries within a country. Most people automatically start judging a person favorably or unfavorably as soon as they detect a speech habit that identifies him with a higher or lower class. "A man's speech," says one British linguist, "refers him to a place in our own system of prejudice." In *Pygmalion*, Henry Higgins says that Eliza's "Kerbstone English will keep her in the gutter to the end of her days." However, reverse snobbery also operates, and in the 19th Century, British aristocrats sometimes affected lower-class speech mannerisms by using such expressions as "ain't."

Several studies demonstrate how people make unconscious assumptions on the basis of class speech habits. In another study, by W. E. Lambert in Montreal in the mid-'60s, a number of Canadians heard tapes in English and in Canadian French. The subjects were asked to describe the speakers in each case. Both French Canadians and English Canadians rated the unseen English-speaker as being more intelligent and dependable, taller, better-looking and kinder than the French-speaker —although both of the recordings had been made by the same bilingual speaker. But the French-speaker was considered to be more benevolent. The results had nothing to do with characteristics of the two languages but merely reflected the social and economic power that was then held by the English-speaking segment of the Canadian population. But, notes Philip S. Dale in a later report, "These attitudes can and do change. French-speaking Canadians have become increasingly concerned with preserving their linguistic heritage."

Class standing affects word usage and grammar as well as pronunciations. Shaw underlined this aspect of behavior in one of the funniest scenes in *Pygmalion*. Eliza, having shucked her Cockney accent under Higgins' tutelage, is enunciating her words with perfect upper-class diction but she is still using the lower-class grammar and vocabulary of Lissom Grove: "Them as pinched it done her in. . . . Them she lived with

In My Fair Lady—a satire on language foibles based on George Bernard Shaw's Pygmalion—aristocratic characters react with horror at a linguistic gaffe. The Cockney flower girl, Eliza Doolittle (center right), forgets all her training in upper-class usage and blurts, "Move your bloomin' arse," to hasten a laggard horse at the Ascot races—thus betraying by her language her plebeian origins.

would have killed her for a hat pin, let alone a hat. . . . If I was doing it proper, what was you laughing at?"

Insecure people who are striving to better themselves often attempt to imitate what they think is the speech of a higher class. A celebrated analysis of such verbal social climbing was provided by philologist Alan Ross and author Nancy Mitford, who compiled a lexicon of U (upper-class) and Non-U (lower-class) words in Britain in the 1950s.

Ross and Mitford listed dozens of pairs of words and phrases that identify speakers by class. In the following examples, Ross and Mitford's U, or upper-class, term is given first, accompanied by the Non-U word: "rich"/"wealthy," "sick"/"ill," "bike"/"cycle," "telegram"/"wire," "house"/"home," "dinner"/"supper," "lunch"/"dinner," "napkin"/"serviette," "what?"/"pardon," "have some more tea"/"how is your cup?" "looking-glass"/"mirror," "jam"/"preserve," "false teeth"/"dentures." The Non-U words generally sound more elegant and fancy, tend to be more indirect and euphemistic, and contain more Latin than Anglo-Saxon roots. The reason is not hard to understand.

Non-U speakers, less confident of their status, try to sound as cultured as they can by mimicking the upper-class speech of an earlier day. Modern U speakers know they are civilized and so they use simpler, more direct terms. An exception to the U fondness for simplicity is a fondness for gross understatement and overstatement. In U speech, a military disaster may be described lightly as a "party," while a party might well be referred to as a "disaster."

Class may mean less linguistically in the United States than it does in Britain, but no one can miss the differences in speech between a factory worker and a corporation president, whatever regional accents they use, and a sharp ear discerns many levels of social status. William Labov studied language patterns among personnel in three department stores in New York City—the fashionable and expensive Saks Fifth Avenue, middle-class Macy's and working-class Klein's—prowling through them like a latter-day Henry Higgins as he tested employees' pronunciations of *r*. New York was once what linguists call an *r*-less area, like Boston, where one still "paaks his caa neah the Haavud Yaad," but Labov found that by the 1960s New Yorkers had come to consider it correct to pronounce final *r*'s and *r*'s that follow vowel sounds. Labov's method was ingenious. In each of the stores he asked scores of employees to give him directions to a department that was located on the fourth floor. Whether they answered "fourth floor" or "fawth flaw," he pretended that he had not heard what they had said, and they would have to repeat the words. Thus each employee had four opportunities to pronounce *r*, two the first time, casually, and two the second time, with emphasis for a customer who did not hear well.

The results were unmistakable. The use of the correct form varied with the status of the store. All four *r*'s were pronounced by 30 per cent of Saks employees and by 20 per cent of Macy's employees but by only 4 per cent of those at Klein's, the plebeian store. At Klein's in fact, where the employees were not fully aware of the prestige attached to the *r* pronunciation, 79 per cent of the staff could manage none of the four *r*'s, while only 38 per cent of those at fashionable Saks were similarly benighted. Labov also heard more *r*'s on the elegant upper floors of Saks than on the crowded ground floor, and more from floorwalkers than from stock boys at Macy's.

Some linguists have suggested that differences between male and female speech are really a form of class distinction, reflecting dominance —male or female—in certain areas of behavior. Japanese feminine speech style is consistently more polite, more indirect, more deferential than masculine speech. Just the opposite is true among the Vakinankaratra of Madagascar, where males speak indirectly and with discretion, and avoid verbal confrontations, while the women employ a more earthy vocabulary to express emotions bluntly. Women do all the haggling in the Vakinankaratra markets, they reprimand children, and they handle all necessary arguments. The menfolk delicately soothe any hurt feelings afterward and take credit as peacemakers. This gentle way of speaking is the admired one among the Vakinankaratra, and the women's plain talk is considered to be a mark of their inferiority.

The most distinctive class language in the United States is the speech of ghetto blacks. For many years Black English was thought to be either a corrupt version of 18th Century English, like the Appalachian dialect, or simply ungrammatical and inarticulate English spoken by people who knew no better. However, linguists now maintain that Black English adheres consistently to a logical syntax of its own, and they have come to the conclusion that its characteristics derive not from ignorance but, like those of any other language, from the history of the people who use it. The difference between the two languages is so great that some linguists believe the two are separate languages.

In support of this point a number of linguists have cited the use of verb tenses in Black English syntax. In Black English not all verbs in a sentence need indicate past or present tense, so long as one of them, or some other word, makes the time clear. But the Black English verb must indicate whether the action is continuous or momentary. William A. Stewart provided what has become the classic example. "My brother sick" means that the brother is sick now but probably not for long. "My brother be sick" means he suffers a long-term illness. Standard English cannot make this precise distinction without additional phrases. Many authorities believe that this type of Black English derives from English and French Creoles, which in turn were based on the English, French and Portuguese pidgins developed by the early slaves, who had to invent ways to communicate with one another because they came from many different African regions and shared no common tongue. Whether Black English is truly a separate language or only a distinct dialect of English, its continued use handicaps ghetto children in white-oriented schools, where standard English is a criterion of a child's performance.

An individual's speech takes on regional and class peculiarities early in life, from family, neighbors and schoolyard playmates. Later when he grows up and goes to work, he often finds that his occupation teaches him new words and ways of speaking that he must adopt in order to do his work properly and to communicate effectively with colleagues. Be-

fore long these new words and phrases become as natural to him as a class-dictated preference for "trousers" or "pants." His occupation has added a new layer of terminology to the personal language he speaks.

The technical terms of any profession are indispensable for precision. "Myringotomy," "habeas corpus" and "anomie" have narrow meanings that surgeons, lawyers and sociologists have difficulty expressing in any other way. The common words "group," "field," "model" and "stability" take on new and very exact meanings when they are used by mathematicians. "Syzygy" is a word used by astronomers, a printer knows that to "bleed" a picture means to let it run to the edge of the page without any margin, and at least seven different trades use the word "go-devil." Among other things, the term can mean a railroad handcar, a sled for hauling logs or the tool that clears obstructions out of oil-well-drilling pipes.

Specialized languages give their users not only precision and economy, but also secrecy—sometimes essential, sometimes self-serving. Doctors use bedside slang to discuss a patient's condition among themselves without letting him hear anything significant: "G.O.K." means "God Only Knows" (what the patient is suffering from). Unscrupulous sales clerks in "borax houses" (stores selling shoddy goods) describe their customers as "J.L." (just looking), "T.O." (to be turned over to an ace salesman), "skank" (cheap skate) or "palooka" (someone on a buying spree). A "palooka" becomes a "wrap-up" if he buys the first item shown, without haggling, and he gets "horned" (overcharged) when he purchases a "skig" or an "L.Y." (last year's goods). All these terms can be used openly in front of the innocent and unsuspecting "proposition" (customer).

If an occupational vocabulary puts a special stamp on the language of professionals, it also affects its users' behavior in another way. More often than not, the arcane words and their special contexts come to symbolize the knowledge, the skills, the shared values and the camaraderie that distinguish the members of the group from the rest of the population. The members begin to use their technical language not just to communicate with one another but to impress the general public, or just to express their solidarity and to make sure that everyone knows who is in and who is out. When a physician calls a "hiccup" a "singultus spasm," and when a policeman refers to the "perpetrator" while telling a television reporter about a "thief," and when a government official "exercises his options" and "introduces innovative techniques" instead of "making a choice" and "trying something new," then the intent is obviously to awe the listener, not to inform him.

This use of professional jargon may have originated with the witch doctor, who fiercely guarded his exclusive authority to speak to the spirits in their own tongue. Today, doctors, priests, engineers, television repairmen, advertising men, skiers, government officials and academics of many persuasions—members of every group that can lay claim to some special learning or authority—defend their lexical turf with similar determination. They can recognize a true colleague by the language he speaks. Anyone who is not a member of their particular group who tries to discuss the specialty will probably give himself away (by not using or by misusing a technical word); at that point the experts will dismiss him as uninformed, regardless of the cogency of his arguments. Journalists are as susceptible as any specialist to this kind of snobbery; let someone talk of a "scoop" nowadays and newsmen will smile condescendingly, for the newer words are "beat" or "exclusive."

Very often a professional's determination to display his erudition and technical competence will lead him into a thicket of jargon so dense that his ideas, if he has any, are obscured. There seems to be no other ex-

planation for the following serious sociological comment on skydiving:

"Within a few moments the highly integrated collectivity that has dominated its individual members (prejump phase) changes drastically into a tenuous, anomic social situation that gives rise to a very egocentric individuality followed by a return to the former state (post-jump phase). This bipolarity of parachuting provides a rare opportunity to study a nearly ideal-typical manifestation of extreme opposite social forms contained within an organizational setting. The sequence of the three phases of the jump and the dialectical relationship between them is analyzed here in terms of personal regression leading to social regression, and vice-versa."

Naturally, when professionals use their technical vocabulary to show off, the public begins to learn what some of the words mean. Outsiders use the special words to pretend they are informed, and the best of the terms creep into the standard language and enrich it. This has been going on since well before the time of Shakespeare and will doubtless continue forever. The gods of mythology crept into the lexicons of astrologers and alchemists, who gave English "jovial," "tantalize,"

In an impromptu salesroom huddle (left), a high-powered auto dealer exhorts his salesmen in the jargon that is as much a mark of their trade as often-satirized technical language is of an academic discipline (right). In the automotive patois "cream puff" means a second-hand car in excellent condition, and "has ice" means it is air conditioned; a "pipe smoker" is a customer who is extremely difficult to sell, and a "tire kicker" is one who is just looking.

"I can't put it into layman's language for you. I don't know any layman's language."

"mercurial," "saturnine" and "protean." From modern military lingo come "jeep," "GI," "gremlin," "task force"; from sports and games, "behind the eight ball," "time out," "knockout," "strike-out," "stymie," "crestfallen," "bluff," "stand pat"; from railroading, "asleep at the switch"; from seafaring, "bilge," "take a new tack," "above-board," "a wide berth," "under the weather," "cut of his jib"; from psychiatry, "complex," "trauma," "fixation" and many more.

The jargon of the space explorers is among the most recent to enter common language, and it introduces a new form. Space engineers, instead of coining new technical terms from Greek and Latin roots, as older sciences did, assembled their specialized vocabulary by putting together long, cumbersome nominal compounds (linguists' jargon for a string of two or more nouns acting as one). In space-speak, the system that controls the attitude of the ship by ejecting gas through nozzles becomes the "nozzle gas ejection ship attitude control system." Psychologist David McNeill of the University of Chicago has calculated that 19 per cent of all the words in official space-agency reports are nominal compounds, a far higher percentage than appears in other scientific writing. One such nominal compound is fully 13 words long: "liquid oxygen liquid hydrogen rocket powered single stage to orbit reversible boost system."

Some of the jargon of space travel, such as "countdown," "hold," "abort" and "destruct," has already become a part of everyday English. "Launching pad" has even taken on a general meaning akin to "basis" or "starting point," as in "never got off the pad."

When region, class and group have left their stamps on an individual's speech he is further influenced by more immediate pressures. Every time he speaks to someone the conventions of society demand that he automatically adjust his language, moment by moment, according to his relationship with those to whom he is speaking. This demand involves two independent aspects of the relationship: the difference in formal status between speaker and listener and the degree of intimacy and familiarity that they enjoy.

The complex honorifics of Japanese provide language for every nuance of rank and status. When speaking to older people, officials, guests, customers, employers or anyone of higher status, the Japanese shift to a set of verb forms that are finely shaded to reflect the precise degree of deference required. A housewife commenting that the weather had improved might say, "Tenki ga yoku narimashita, ne," to a neighbor lady of equal status; she would say, "Tenki ga yoroshu narimashita desu, ne," to an older woman acquaintance; and then she would have to say,

Playing the horses at Britain's Epsom track, bettors and bookies carry out their business in a colorful argot, derived from Cockney slang, that identifies them as members of the racing fraternity. A bookie refers to a customer as a "punter"; a big-money player might wager a "pony" (£25) or even a "monkey" (£500).

"Tenki ga yoku narimashita de gozaimasu, ne," to the principal of the local school. With each more deferential form her bows of greeting and departure would become deeper and longer.

Paralleling the many words for "I," the Japanese also have several words for the pronoun "you," some to aim at inferiors and others for equals of various kinds. But when talking to someone of significantly higher status, an employer for instance, no word for "you" is good enough; instead, the Japanese use the title, or the name plus the honorific suffix, *-san*. For instance, they will not ask the section chief, "Have you seen this report?" but "Has section chief seen this report?"

Every bit as important as status to the Japanese is the sense of belonging to a family, a company or some other group, and another set of rules is needed to express this relationship or the lack of it. A Japanese refers to his own house, or the house of a close relative, as "uchi," but the house of the person he is speaking to is "otaku." The basic word for daughter is "musume," but it is used only when referring to one's own daughter or to a daughter who somehow belongs to the speaker's in-group; the listener's daughter—assuming the listener belongs to a different family or group—or the daughter of a third person of equal rank, is "ojosan." Outside the family, Japanese males express the spirit of group solidarity by adding the suffix *-kun* to the names of close friends instead of using the more distant and formal suffix *-san*. However, females in Japan have no way of indicating this form of camaraderie because traditionally they are not supposed to have close friends or interests outside their homes.

The intricate Japanese system has at least one advantage: the rules, once absorbed, are quite clear and specific. As long as the Japanese know whom they are talking to, they seldom have difficulty choosing the proper level of speech. Most Americans think that their own system is simple and democratic, but in a way it is more difficult to master because the rules are flexible and often ambiguous.

The ambiguity in the American system lies in the fact that the two fundamental aspects of a relationship, status and intimacy, are both involved with what is essentially the same decision, whether to address a person by the first name ("Frank") or by a title and the last name ("Mr. Jones"). An American may say "Mr. Smith" to a nodding acquaintance as well as to a boss with whom he has worked for years; and he may say "Bill" to a long-time friend as well as to a subordinate whom he barely knows.

Where status is equal, or where status is ignored as at an informal party, intimacy becomes the governing factor; most Americans will progress rather quickly from the more formal "Mr. Jones" to the mutual use of first names. According to psychologists Roger Brown and Marguerite Ford, who conducted extensive studies of address forms in many situations, younger people and persons of the same sex first-name each other most readily. Shared values, a degree of honest self-disclosure and frequent contact seem to be necessary for first-name intimacy in all Western languages, but among Americans the switch to the use of first names can take place after as little as five minutes of conversation—a practice that Europeans visiting the United States find quite difficult to get accustomed to.

Unequal status, of course, changes the picture. The person of highest status always makes the first move; when sufficient familiarity has been established he will start calling his subordinate by first name, leaving the subordinate to decide if and when he dare return the gesture. This unequal pattern may last forever. Brown and Ford believe that the higher status individual sets the pace in order to spare his subordinate the risk of rebuff; presumably no one will ever object to being first-named by his boss, but the boss might well resent a premature "Hi, Joe," from the office boy. Sometimes a shift in naming patterns reflects a subtle change in relationship: some American doctors address their patients as "Mr. Smith" until Mr. Smith is old enough to have his bills paid by Medicare; then he becomes "John."

How easily an individual can make the switch to two-way first-naming may depend on his rank. A study of one San Francisco insurance company showed that the top managers and the lower-level personnel were more casual about first-naming their superiors than were the people in the middle ranks; it was the middle-level supervisors who took longer to call their bosses by first name. This study also indicated that most people are uncomfortable with the unequal naming pattern when a boss is younger than his employee. Pairs of individuals in that awkward situation either held on to the formal style of "Mr. Smith" or "Mr. Jones" longer than others did or else they progressed more quickly to use of first names in both directions.

The most distant and respectful form of address is to use a title only, as in "Sir," "Ma'am," "Colonel," "Officer," "Doctor" or "Professor." At the other end of the scale, and even more intimate than two-way first-naming, is the practice of calling a good friend by a free variety of names and nicknames to match the mood of the moment. According to Brown and Ford, multiple names for intimates are like the dozen terms the Eskimos have for the word "snow": they are a sign of importance and concern to the speaker.

All these customs may seem just natural to most speakers of a language but they actually make up a set of unwritten rules whose implications are generally understood. This becomes evident when someone deliberately violates the rules in order to deliver an insult. Alvin Poussaint, a black psychiatrist, reported the following highly charged dialogue between a Southern policeman and himself:

"What's your name, boy?"
"Dr. Poussaint. I'm a physician."
"What's your first name, boy?"
"Alvin."

The policeman insulted Poussaint four times in the course of this short exchange: first by calling him "boy," the outmoded white term for black males of any age; next by ignoring a general rule of address for physicians; then by insisting on learning Poussaint's first name, with the implication that he had a right to use it; and finally by calling him "boy" again. Poussaint reported that he experienced "profound humiliation" as he gave the policeman his first name and thereby helplessly accepted the insult.

In most European languages the degree of intimacy between speakers is expressed by the second person pronoun. The pronoun is used to distinguish social relationships: "tu" and "vous" in French, "du" and "Sie" in German, and "tu" and "Lei" in Italian. According to some linguists, the plural form was first used to show respect during the Fourth Century, when the Roman Empire was split and two emperors reigned, one in Rome and one in Constantinople. Anything spoken to one of them was regarded as having been addressed to both, so the plural form, "vos" in Latin, became obligatory when addressing the emperor. (Another theory is that the emperor was considered plural simply because he represented the sum of his people.) The use of "vos" to the emperor was gradually extended to include other persons of higher status and by the 13th Century, in many countries of Europe, superiors addressed inferiors as "tu" (singular) and the inferiors used "vos" ("vous" in French) when they were speaking even to one superior. Between equals, the upper classes used the plural—probably because they were the ones who addressed the kings—and the lower classes used the "tu" form.

But the French Revolution undermined the concept of social caste. During the 19th Century, Europeans began to resent the inequality of the old forms of address. They were no longer willing to say "vous" to someone who said "tu" to them, and they developed a new egalitarian pattern in which both members of a pair used the same pronoun to each other. This pattern is based on intimacy, or solidarity, the sense of like-mindedness growing out of family ties or shared experiences. In the new and modern usage the plural form "vous" continues to signify distance, but now it is more the horizontal distance between strangers—not the vertical distance of status.

Today speakers of French, German, Italian, Spanish, Portuguese, Russian and several other languages use the "tu" form to close friends and kin, and say "vous" to anyone outside the intimate circle. Whichever form two people may decide to use, they both use the same form. Vestiges of the status pattern have survived to recent times, however. Up to World War II at least, Yiddish pronoun usage had still not completely shifted. Jewish family members all said "du" to each other

Queen Elizabeth II is properly greeted (as "Your Majesty") by Mrs. Harold Wilson.

Fancy labels
for high offices

THE QUEEN
Envelope: The Queen's Most Excellent
　Majesty
Letter: May it please your Majesty
Speech: Your Majesty

THE DUKE OF BEDFORD
Envelope: His Grace the Duke of Bedford
Letter: My Lord Duke
Speech: Your Grace

THE MARCHIONESS OF TAVISTOCK
Envelope: The Most Hon. Marchioness of
　Tavistock
Letter: Madam
Speech: Your Ladyship

THE ARCHBISHOP OF CANTERBURY
Envelope: The Most Reverend the Lord
　Archbishop of Canterbury
Letter: My Lord Archbishop
Speech: Your Grace

THE DEAN OF ST. PAUL'S CATHEDRAL
Envelope: The Very Reverend the Dean of St.
　Paul's
Letter: Very Reverend Dean
Speech: Mr. Dean

THE LORD MAYOR OF BIRMINGHAM
Envelope: The Right Worshipful the Lord
　Mayor of Birmingham
Letter: My Lord; My Lord Mayor
Speech: Sir

How to talk to
the upper class

When Sir W. S. Gilbert, in his libretto for *The Mikado*, described Ko-Ko as "Lord High Executioner of Titipu," and Pooh-Bah as "Lord High Everything Else," he was trying to parody the human penchant for pompous titles. But Gilbert's parody seems pale beside reality, for man's addiction to fancy titles and deferential modes of address takes some comic forms.

The British, in particular, are sticklers for precise and proper forms of address. For every occasion and for every medium—on an envelope, in a letter or in person—there are special words to be used, different ones for queens *(above)*, dukes, marchionesses, clergymen and politicians.

Protocol specifies the permutations of address for a noble lady before and after marriage. For example, the daughter of a duke, even as a child, might be called "The Lady Mary Smith" on an envelope, "Madam" on the letter inside, and "Your Ladyship" in speech. If she eventually married Viscount Arbuthnott, the envelope address would change to "The Viscountess Arbuthnott." If she ran off and married the gardener's son, she would retain her honorific titles and be known as "The Lady Mary Jones," wife of plain "Mr. Jones."

regardless of their age, but outside the family, persons of status (older, wealthier, more learned) often were addressed "ir" (the plural) and said "du" downward. Moreover, the European memory of the old status pattern makes it now very bad taste to say "tu" to a waiter, for that would be an undemocratic reminder of his lowly occupation.

But it is still the person of higher status who retains the right to suggest the change from mutual "vous" to mutual "tu." The timing of that shift varies from country to country and group to group. French mountaineers start using "tu" to each other when they climb above a critical altitude. Studies show that Germans are more likely to use "du" to distant relatives than are the French, suggesting that family ties may be stronger in Germany. Italian male students use "tu" more readily to female students—especially if the females are attractive—than French or German students do. In France today young people regard almost any shared activity as grounds for using "tu."

The change-over to the intimate form is an important milestone in the relationship between any two Europeans and once the shift is made, it is rarely reversed. When the delicate moment to change from "Sie" to "du" approaches, the Germans act out a little ceremony, called "Brüderschaft trinken" ("drinking to brotherhood"). On a congenial, mellow occasion, over a glass of wine, the senior will suggest the change, the junior will agree, and they will link arms and drink to their new linguistic solidarity.

How language and behavior affect each other depends mainly on the situation. The same speaker, addressing the same listeners, will talk (and act) differently under different circumstances. A web of unwritten conventions governs what can be said—and by whom—in almost every kind of confrontation between people. The average person is seldom aware of them, despite the fact that he is adjusting his speech at every moment to the circumstances he is in. A postman or a doorman speaks differently when he takes off his uniform; a clerk behind the counter of a store feels protected from personal remarks—and is expected to avoid uttering any; children learn early to shift from nursery style, where certain words for bodily functions are permissible, to the dinner-table style —especially when guests are present. The precise rules that apply in each case, the words and grammar and tone of voice that will and will not be acceptable in a given context or situation, vary from region to region, from class to class and from country to country, but they do exist everywhere. Those who violate the rules do so to their shame—or for dramatic effect.

Many of the rules concern the fitness of topics. No one tells dirty sto-

The life and death of words

Languages have a life of their own: old words die and new ones are born. The American colonists of 1775 would have understood all of the words in the column at right. Today most are dead, although some have simply changed their forms. All of the words at far right have emerged since the time of the colonists. "Boondocks," for example, is from the Philippine word "bundok," for "mountain," and was brought back to the United States by Marines of World War II. "Maverick" was the name of a Texan who let his calves run free without putting his brand on them.

18TH CENTURY ENGLISH		MODERN AMERICAN WORDS
bespawl	to spit on	blizzard
brangle	quarrel	boondocks
compromit	to pledge	bottleneck
congrue	to fit together	cheap skate
foisty	musty	cliff-hanger
gimmer	ewe	crackdown
glede	askew	double cross
grubble	to grope	gimmick
ingeny	wit	gobbledygook
jeopard	to endanger	hobo
jugulate	to cut the throat of	jaywalk
kickshoe	a buffoon	know-how
nuncheon	snack	lynch
pillowbeer	a pillow slip	maverick
pinker	to squint	nostalgia
potch	to thrust or push	smooch
yarrish	to have a rough, dry taste	stampede
yux	to hiccup	tycoon

ries in church or speaks in loud tones at the bedside of a sick person. Some hostesses ban from their dinner tables the discussion of politics and religion, or any other subjects that would be likely to provide grounds for an argument.

Even the most casual encounters are subject to strict regulation. In an English-speaking situation, a request to a stranger for information is generally preceded by a polite apology, and nothing more: "Excuse me. Could you tell me how to get to the post office?" A conversational gambit that started out, "Hello, my name is Joe Smith and I come from Wisconsin," is unlikely to be followed by a simple request like "What time is it?" The stranger who introduces himself is expected to have more serious business in mind. In the American West, two people who find themselves sitting next to each other on a bus will probably strike up a friendly, casual conversation within a few minutes, especially if they are of the same age and sex. However, if one of them were to attempt the same type of casual conversation in New York, where silence between strangers is acceptable social behavior, he might make his seatmate decidedly uncomfortable.

There is also a fundamental difference between the style of a speech or a monologue and the style of a conversation. When two people are holding a dialogue each helps the other along by gestures, by expressions of understanding, and by filling out sentences when his companion is groping for words. Consequently neither speaker need complete every thought. But a public speaker on a dais gets little specific feedback from his audience. He can tell whether his listeners are enthusiastic or bored, but if he wants to be sure they understand him he must round out

every point and even repeat some of them. This shift in style and tone is most noticeable when a minister finishes his sermon and starts to chat with his parishioners at the church door. A public speaker, moreover, will sprinkle his delivery with jokes, will pronounce his words more carefully than he does in private speech (he may pronounce more final *g*'s for instance) and he will go through a ritual of telling his listeners how happy he is to be with them.

Civility dictates many forms of expression. For example, "you may" is usually more polite than "you should," which is much more polite than "you must." But if a hostess at an American dinner party says, "You must try some of this," she is being more polite than if she said, "You should try some of this" or "You may try some of this." The last phrase in that situation is aloof and unfriendly, but a foreign guest who had studied his verbs might mistakenly prefer it to the first.

The Japanese are masters at polite indirection. In informal, ordinary discourse the Japanese can say simply, "He came home." A more formal situation demands a phrase meaning roughly, "The fact of his return happened." And if local politicians are announcing the return of their leader, they might say softly, "He has become visible." When the situation really gets stiff, the Japanese shift to a special set of honorific verbs that mean nothing more than the common verbs like "come," "go," "talk," "eat," or "to be," but which carry a whole cargo of deference and indirection. These honorific verbs are distinct from and more polite than the polite forms of ordinary verbs.

Formality generally contains an element of ritual, and ritual phrases are common in almost every language. The English, "How do you do," "Pleased to meet you," "The pleasure is mine," "I wonder if you could . . .," may be relics of a more ceremonial era in the history of the language. In many of the Southwest Pacific islands today, every important village occasion must be marked with a drinking bout at which carefully prescribed speech forms are required from every participant. In the hospitable Fiji version of this practice, an expert talker may be assigned to sit by and speak for a foreigner, who does not know the forms. The Subanum people of Mindanao in the Philippines choose their political leaders and their judges through competitive drinking-and-talking bouts that follow a stylized format. The object of the game is to secure as many responses as possible to one's own utterances, while discussing precisely delimited topics at each stage. In the course of the ceremony, disputes are settled and status is redistributed to those who display great verbal prowess.

All the social pressures on the individual, interacting with his per-

When humorist Lenny Bruce performed in a London cabaret in 1962 (right), his obscene assaults on religion and social mores drew critical acclaim—although some spectators walked out and others even threw bottles. Bruce's liberal use of four-letter words later led to his deportation from England. Barred from performing in Canada and often arrested in the United States, he was convicted in 1964 of obscenity in New York during a trial that ultimately destroyed his career.

Language that is off limits

Zuñi Indians are as shocked to hear their word for bean spoken aloud at a religious gathering as nightclub audiences were to hear the obscenities that peppered the performances of humorist Lenny Bruce *(above)*. The reason why "bean" offends the Zuñi is obscure, but every society has its quota of language that is considered unacceptable.

One authority on folklore, Gershon Legman, has observed national variations in obscenity in Western societies. His conclusions are likely to provoke debate, but he believes that Dutch and German dirty jokes often deal with excretion; amiable seduction, adultery and sexual techniques dominate French off-color humor; American jokes focus upon oral-genital themes and the debasement of women, while Britons banter about homosexuality and incest.

Why do people feel a need to use of-

fensive language? Freud suggested that obscenity is a subconscious tool of sexual seduction. Other psychologists have theorized that obscenity is a way to draw attention to the speaker and to mock authority figures. Obscene language has even been the focus of social rebellion. During the 1964 so-called Free Speech riots at the University of California, students symbolized their protest with signs bearing four-letter words (and opponents called the protesters the Filthy Speech Movement).

In retaliation, societies punish those who violate the standards of obscenity with sanctions that range from disapproval and ostracism to imprisonment. Works of literature like D. H. Lawrence's *Lady Chatterley's Lover* have been suppressed, and Lenny Bruce was repeatedly prosecuted for his obscene performances.

sonality and his unique experiences, combine to produce a manner of speaking that is his alone. If two middle-class boys were brought up on the same block in a small city in Ohio they would speak with the same flat twang and neither could be mistaken for a native of New York or Atlanta. But if the parents of one of them are recent immigrants, he may tend to speak just a little bit more formally to older people than the boy down the block.

Later if one of the boys then goes away to a university in Boston, stays in New England to become a professor of sociology, and marries a woman who is from a smart Philadelphia suburb, his speech may absorb some Eastern regionalisms. He may stop saying "strange" for "shy," for example, and he may refer to a "small paper bag" and a "sack of potatoes" instead of a "small paper sack" and a "bag of potatoes." He will fall easily into his academic jargon, and his readiness to call an older colleague by his first name, Tom, instead of addressing him as "Professor Smith" will depend on the prevailing customs of his college. At the same time, influenced by his wife, he may relax in the "living room" instead of in the "parlor."

Meanwhile his boyhood friend has served a hitch in the Air Force, attended school in Texas and become a computer programmer for a large corporation that transfers him to a different city every two or three years. He may say "negative" for "no," and "howdy" for "hello," and he may speak more slowly. If his television set does not work, he will say it is "down," not "out of order."

Twenty years after the two men finished high school a linguist with a good ear might still be able to identify the region they came from, but if the two men meet it will be apparent to each of them that social pressures have altered the other's manner of speaking. The tone of voice, vocabulary and stress patterns, pauses and rhythms, and range of pitch —all these characteristics combine to make their personal speech styles recognizable to all who know them in their new environments.

Personal speech sometimes narrows down to a phrase or two that become trademarks of identity. In England, according to the author Evelyn Waugh, one snobbish lady's unmistakable phrase of scorn was, "Rather MIF, darling," the "MIF" standing for "milk in first," an abhorrent, juvenile way of making tea. A personal, easily recognized style of speech is so memorable and impressive that no public figure, and especially no politician, can afford to be without one. Such is the power of these hallmarks of private speech that few Americans need be reminded who wanted to "make one thing perfectly clear"; and no middle-aged American can forget who owned the simple phrase, "My friends. . . ."

Worlds Shaped by Words

5

The scene is the storage room at a chemical plant. The time is evening. A night watchman enters the room and notes that it is partially filled with gasoline drums. The drums are in a section of the room where a sign says, "Empty Barrels." The watchman lights a cigarette and throws the still-hot match into one of the empty barrels.

The result: an explosion.

The immediate cause of the explosion, of course, was the gasoline fumes that remained in the barrels. But it could be argued that a second cause of the explosion was the English language. The barrels were empty of their original contents and so belonged under the empty sign. Yet they were not empty of everything—the fumes were still present. English has no word—no single term—that can convey such a situation. Containers in English are either empty or they are not; there is no word describing the ambiguous state of being empty and yet not empty. There is no term in the language for "empty but not quite" or "empty of original contents but with something left over." There being no word for such an in-between state, it did not occur to the watchman to think of the explosive fumes.

This incident is hypothetical, but the questions about language it raises are real. The example of the gasoline drums often was cited by Benjamin Lee Whorf as an example to illustrate a revolutionary theory he had about language. Whorf was an unusual man who combined two careers, for he was both a successful insurance executive and a brilliant (and largely self-taught) linguistic scholar. Language, he claimed, may be shaped by the world, but it in turn shapes the world. He reasoned that people can think about only those things that their language can describe or express. Without the words or structures with which to articulate a concept, that concept will not occur. To turn the proposition around, if a language is rich in ways to express certain sorts of ideas, then the speakers of that language will habitually think along those linguistic paths. In short, the language that a man speaks governs his view of reality, it determines his perception of the world. The picture of the universe shifts from tongue to tongue.

The originator of this startling notion came from an intellectually active New England family. Whorf's brother John became an artist of note and his brother Richard a consummately professional actor. Benjamin's early bent was not for drawing or acting but photography, especially the chemistry that was involved in developing pictures, and this interest may have influenced his choice of the Massachusetts Institute of Technology, where he majored in chemical engineering. After he was graduated from M.I.T. he became a specialist in fire prevention and in 1919 went to work for the Hartford Fire Insurance Company, his job being to inspect manufacturing plants, particularly chemical plants, that the Hartford insured to determine whether they were safe and thus good insurance risks. He quickly became highly skilled at his work. "In no time at all," wrote C. S. Kremer, then the Hartford's board chairman, "he became in my opinion as thorough and fast a fire prevention inspector as there ever has been."

Whorf was a particularly acute chemical engineer. On one occasion he was refused admittance to inspect a client's building because, a company official maintained, a secret process was in use there. "You are making such-and-such a product?" asked Whorf. "Yes," said the official. Whorf pulled out a pad and scribbled the formula of the supposedly secret process, adding coolly, "You couldn't do it any other way." Needless to say, he was allowed to inspect the building. Whorf rose in the Hartford hierarchy to the post of assistant secretary of the company in 1940. But then in 1941 his health, never strong, gave way, and he died at the early age of 44.

While Whorf was becoming a successful insurance executive, he was also doing his revolutionary work in linguistics. He started by studying Hebrew but then switched to Aztec and other related languages of Mexico. Later he deciphered Maya inscriptions, and tried to reconstruct the long-lost language of the ancient Maya people of Mexico and Central America. Finally he tackled the complexities of the still-living language of the Hopi Indians of Arizona. He published his findings in respected anthropological and linguistic journals, earning the praise and respect of scholars in the two fields—all without formal training in linguistic science. As his fame as a linguist spread, the Hartford obligingly afforded him vacations and leaves to travel to the Southwest in pursuit of the structure and lexicon of the Hopi. He also put in countless hours in the Watkinson Library in Connecticut, a rich repository of Mexican and Indian lore.

Benjamin Lee Whorf, the innovative linguist, looks the model of a successful insurance executive—which he also was. Whorf combined the two careers while he developed his controversial ideas about the impact of language on people's view of the world around them.

It was primarily his study of Hopi that impelled Whorf toward his revolutionary ideas. He was encouraged and aided by the great cultural anthropologist and linguist of Yale, Edward Sapir, and the idea that language influences a man's view of the world is generally known as the Sapir-Whorf hypothesis. Whorf formulated it a number of times, but perhaps his clearest statement comes from his 1940 essay "Science and Linguistics": "The background linguistic system (in other words, the grammar) of each language is not merely a reproducing instrument for voicing ideas but rather is itself the shaper of ideas. . . . We dissect nature along lines laid down by our native language. The categories and types that we isolate from the world of phenomena we do not find there because they stare every observer in the face; on the contrary, the world is presented in a kaleidoscopic flux of impressions which has to be organized by our minds—and this means largely by the linguistic systems in our minds."

These ideas developed from Whorf's study of the Hopi language. He discovered that it differs dramatically from languages of the Indo-European family such as English or French, particularly in its expression of the concept of time. English and its sister languages have three major tenses, past, present and future—"it was," "it is," "it will be" —plus the fancier compound tenses such as "it will have been." Having these tenses, Whorf argued, encourages Europeans and Americans to think of time as so many ducks in a row. Time past is made up of uniform units of time—days, weeks, months, years—and the future is similarly measured out. This division of time is essentially artificial, Whorf said, since people can only experience the present. Past and future are only abstractions, but Westerners think of them as real because their language virtually forces them to do so. This view of time has given rise to the fondness in Western cultures for diaries, records, annals, histories, clocks, calendars, wages paid by the hour or day, and elaborate timetables for the use of future time. Time is continually quantified. If Westerners set out to build a house they establish a deadline; the work will be completed at a specified time in the future such as May 5 or October 15.

A Hopi does not behave this way—when he starts to weave a mat he is not concerned about when it will be completed. He works on it desultorily, then quits, then begins again; the finished product may take weeks. This casual progress is not laziness but a result of the Hopi's view of time—one symptom of the fact that his language does not have the past, present and future tenses. Instead it possesses two modes of thought, the objective, that is, things that exist now, and the subjective,

An Umingmagtormiut Eskimo from the far northern Bathurst Bay west of Hudson's Bay area adjusts the sled harness on a Husky wearing canvas boots to protect its paws from "masa"—wet spring snow. This kind of snow softens paws so that ice easily cuts into them.

"Oqaalugait," hard packed snow that is of the right consistency to be cut into house-building blocks, is used to make an igloo near Bathurst Bay. Eskimos also use the term for igloo snow to mean "north"—igloos always face north.

The Eskimo's many words for snow

An Eskimo woman drops chunks of soft snow, called "pukajaq," into her teapot while a befurred child looks on. The ability to recognize snow that will be suitable for cooking and for drinking is the mark of a good housewife.

There is only one word in English for snow, a substance that has been mainly a nuisance to those who helped shape the language, although several terms —"hail," "sleet," "glare ice"—distinguish frozen rain that endangers crops or transport. Hail or sleet are of little concern to Eskimos, but snow is another matter. Among tribes like the Umingmagtormiut shown here, there are a dozen basic words for snow.

By adding suffixes to the words for snow, the Umingmagtormiut can make more than a hundred fine distinctions, describing consistency and indicating whether snow is on the ground, falling or blowing. There is a special word for wind-driven snow, "tiqsiq," and another, "tuva," for snow atop ice. With this range of terminology, Eskimos can discuss with great subtlety the natural substance that most affects their lives.

things that can be thought about and therefore belong to a state of be-coming. Things do not become in terms of a future measured off in days, weeks, months. Each thing that is becoming has its own individual life rhythms, growing or declining or changing in much the same man-ner as a plant grows, according to its inner nature. The essence of Hopi life therefore, Whorf said, is preparing in the present so that those things that are capable of becoming can in fact come to pass. Thus weaving a mat is preparing a mat to become a mat; it will reach that state when its nature so ordains—whenever that will be.

This view of the future is understandable, Whorf noted, in an ag-ricultural people whose welfare depends on the proper preparing of earth and seeds and plants for the hoped-for harvest. It also helps ex-plain why the Hopi have such elaborate festivals, rituals, dances and magic ceremonies: All are intended to aid in the mental preparation that is so necessary if the crops, which the Hopi believe to be influenced by human thought, are to grow properly. This preparing involves "much visible activity," Whorf said, "introductory formalities, preparing of special food . . . intensive sustained muscular activity like running, rac-ing, dancing, which is thought to increase the intensity of development of events (such as growth of crops), mimetic and other magic prepa-rations based on esoteric theory involving perhaps occult instruments like prayer sticks, prayer feathers, and prayer meal, and finally the great cyclic ceremonies and dances, which have the significance of pre-paring rain and crops." Whorf went on to note that the very noun for "crop" is derived from the verb that means "to prepare." "Crop" there-fore is in the Hopi language literally "the prepared." Further, the Hopi prayer pipe, which is smoked as an aid in concentrating good thoughts on the growing fields of corn and wheat, is named "na'twanpi," "in-strument of preparing."

The past to the Hopi, Whorf believed, is also different from the chro-nological time sense of the speakers of Indo-European languages. The past is not a uniform row of days or weeks to the Hopi. It is rather an un-differentiated stream in which many deeds were done that have accumulated and prepared the present and will continue to prepare the becoming that is ahead. Everything is connected, everything accumu-lates. The past is not a series of events, separated and completed, but is present in the present.

To Whorf these striking differences in the Hopi language and sense of time implied that the Hopi live almost literally in another world from the speakers of Indo-European languages. The Hopi language grew out of its speakers' peculiar circumstances: As a geographically isolated agricultural people in a land where rainfall was scanty, they did the same things and prayed the same prayers year after year and thus did not need to have past and future tenses. But the language, once it had developed, perpetuated their particular and seemingly very different world view.

Many linguists and anthropologists who have worked with American Indians of the Southwest have been convinced that Whorf's theories are by and large correct. Other linguists are not convinced, however, and through the years since Whorf's death they have attacked his proposals. The controversy is unlikely to be settled soon, if ever. One of the problems is the difficulty of setting up an experiment that would either prove or disprove the existence of correlations between linguistic structure and nonlinguistic behavior. It would be fruitless to go about asking people of various cultures their opinions as to whether the language they spoke had determined the manner in which they thought, had dictated their view of the world. Nobody would be able to answer such a question, for a person's language is so completely embedded in his consciousness that he would be unable to conceive of any other way of interpreting the world.

Despite the near impossibility of proving or disproving Whorf's theory, it will not go away but keeps coming back, intriguing each succeeding generation of linguists. It is certainly one of the most fascinating theories created by the modern mind. It is comparable in some ways to Einstein's theory of relativity. Just as Einstein said that how a person saw the phenomena of the universe was relative to his point of observation, so Whorf said that a person's world view was relative to the language he spoke.

And demonstrations of Whorf's ideas are not entirely lacking. They come mainly from studies of color—one of the very few aspects of reality that can be specified by objective scientific methods and also is rather precisely specified by peoples' naming of colors. In this instance it is possible to compare one person's language, expressing his view of the world, with another's language for exactly the same characteristic of the world. The comparison can thus reveal different views that are linked to different descriptions of the same reality. English-speakers view purple as a single relatively uniform color; only if pressed and then only with difficulty will they make any attempt to divide it into such shades as lavender and mauve. But no English-speaker would lump orange with purple; to the users of English, those colors are completely separate, for no single word includes both of them. If other languages made

The pivotal role of language in shaping a society is demonstrated in these two classrooms. In Israel (left), adults from many lands study Hebrew, learning the common tongue that is the basis for a national culture. The United States, once insistent on a single language, now favors diversity. In the bilingual class above, in Beacon, New York, Spanish-speaking children learn English while retaining their ancestral tongue—and culture.

different distinctions in the naming of color—if lavender and mauve were always separate, never encompassed by a word for purple, or if orange and purple were not distinguished but were called by a name that covered both—then it would seem that the users of those languages interpreted those colors differently.

Such differences in color-naming, it turns out, are fairly widespread. Linguist H. A. Gleason compared the color spectrum as described by English-speaking persons to the way it was labeled by speakers of Bassa, a language spoken in Liberia, and by speakers of Shona, spoken in Rhodesia. English-speaking people, when seeing sunlight refracted through a prism, identify by name at least six colors—purple, blue, green, yellow, orange and red. The speakers of Shona, however, have only three names for the colors of the spectrum. They group orange, red and purple under one name. They also lump blue and green-blue under one of their other color terms and use their third word to identify yellow and the yellower hues of green. The speakers of Bassa are similarly restricted by a lack of handy terms for color, for they have only two words for the hues of the spectrum.

Gleason's observations prompted psychologists to perform an experiment that also showed the influence words can have on the way colors are handled intellectually and remembered. It was an ingenious and complex experiment with many checks and double checks of the results, but in essence it boiled down to something like this: English-speaking subjects were shown a series of color samples—rather like the little "chips" provided by a paint store to help customers decide what color to paint the living room. The subjects were then asked to pick out the colors they had seen from a far larger array of colors. It turned out that they could more accurately pick out the right colors from the larger selection when the color involved had a handy, ordinary name like "green." The subjects had difficulty with the ambiguous, in-between colors such as off-purples and misty blues. In other words, a person can remember a color better if his language offers a handy label for it, and he has trouble when the language does not offer such a familiar term. Again the human ability to differentiate reality seemed to be affected by the resources offered by language.

Richness of linguistic resource undoubtedly helps people to cope with subtle gradations in the things they deal with every day. The Hanunóo people of the Philippine Islands have different names for 92 varieties of rice. They can easily distinguish differences in rice that would be all but invisible to English-speaking people, who lump all such grains under the single word "rice." Of course, English-speakers can make distinctions by resorting to adjectives and perhaps differentiate long-grain, brown rice from small-grain, yellow rice, but surely no European or American would, lacking the terms, have a sufficiently practiced eye to distinguish 92 varieties of rice. Language is essentially a code that people use both to think and to communicate. As psychologist Roger Brown sums up the rice question: "Among the Hanunóo, who have names for ninety-two varieties of rice, any one of those varieties is highly codable in the array of ninety-one other varieties. The Hanunóo have a word for it and so can transmit it efficiently and presumably can recognize it easily. Among speakers of English one kind of rice among ninety-one other kinds would have very low codability."

Brown goes on to suppose that the Hanunóo set down in New York would be baffled by the reality around them partly because they would then be the ones lacking the needed words. "If the Hanunóo were to visit the annual Automobile Show in New York City, they would find it difficult to encode distinctively any particular automobile in that array.

But an American having such lexical resources as *Chevrolet, Ford, Plymouth, Buick, Corvette, hard-top, convertible, four-door, station wagon,* and the like could easily encode ninety-two varieties."

The very existence of so many different languages, each linked to a distinctive culture, is itself support of a sort for Whorf's hypothesis. At least since the time of the Tower of Babel, no single tongue has been shared by all the people of the world. Many attempts have been made to invent an international language, one so simply structured and easy to learn it would be used by everyone around the globe as a handy adjunct to his native speech. Yet even the most successful of these world languages, Esperanto *(overleaf)*, has found but limited acceptance.

There are international languages, however, to serve international cultures. The intellectual disciplines of music, dance and mathematics might be considered specialized cultures; each is shared by people around the world, and each has an international language, used as naturally in Peking as in Paris. English is a world language in certain activities that straddle national boundaries, such as international air travel; it serves for communications between international flights and the ground in every country—a Lufthansa pilot approaching Athens talks with the airport control tower neither in German nor in Greek but in English.

The trouble with most attempts to lend credence to the Sapir-Whorf hypothesis is that, while they indicate connections between culture and language, they do not really prove that a language shaped its users' view of the world. Just because the speakers of Shona have only three main distinctions of color does not mean that their "world view" is all that different from that of the English-speaker who has more convenient color terms. Shona speakers obviously see all the colors in the rainbow that English-speakers see. Their eyes are physiologically the same. Their comparative poverty of words for those colors merely means that it is harder for them to talk about color. Their "code" is not so handy; the colors' codability is lower.

Critics also point out that Whorf may have mistaken what are called dead metaphors for real differences in the Hopi language. All languages are loaded with dead metaphors—figures of speech that have lost all figurative value and are now just familiar words. The word "goodbye" is a dead metaphor. Once it meant "God be with you," but in its contracted form it conjures up no thought or picture of God. If a Whorfian linguist who was a native speaker of Hopi turned the tables and analyzed English he might conclude that English-speakers were perpet-

Ludwik Zamenhof, creator of Esperanto, was born in a Polish town where Poles, Russians, Germans and Jews all spoke their own tongues. He believed that language differences are "the principal cause of disunity in the human family."

A tongue for all nations: Esperanto

The idea of a universal language has always tempted men. In the 1870s, a brilliant multilingual Polish teenager, Ludwik Zamenhof, began to devise a solution: a simple language with a skeletal grammar and a vocabulary, largely derived from the Romance languages.

In 1887, when he was just 27, Zamenhof published his work under a pseudonym, Doktoro Esperanto ("Doctor Hopeful"), that gave his creation its name. Esperanto is simple: a flyer promoting it explains the fundamentals in one page *(right)*. The language has proved adaptable and resilient. Though not a true lingua franca, it is spoken by hundreds of thousands of people and used in over 10,000 books.

Esperanto at a Glance

The Alphabet of Esperanto

A a	B b	C c	Ĉ ĉ	D d
ah	*bo*	*tso*	*cho*	*do*
E e	F f	G g	Ĝ ĝ	H h
eh	*fo*	*go*	*Joe*	*ho*
Ĥ ĥ	I i	J j	Ĵ ĵ	K k
hho	*ee*	*yo*	*zho*	*ko*
L l	M m	N n	O o	
lo	*mo*	*no*	*oh*	
P p	R r	S s	Ŝ ŝ	T t
po	*ro*	*so*	*sho*	*toe*
U u	Ŭ ŭ	V v	Z z	
oo	*woe*	*vo*	*zo*	

28 Letters. There is no Q, W, X, or Y.

A, E, I, O, U have approximately the vowel sounds heard in *bar, bear, beer, bore, boor.*

C is not sounded like S or K, but like *ts* in Tsar.

J has the sound of *y* in *yes.*

The sounds of ĉ, ĝ, ĥ, ĵ, ŝ, and ŭ are heard in *leech, liege, loch, leisure, leash,* and *leeway.*

ESPERANTO IS PHONETIC.

All letters sounded: one letter one sound.

ACCENT or STRESS falls on the last syllable but one.

No IRREGULARITIES.   No EXCEPTIONS.

THE GRAMMAR is based upon SIXTEEN FUNDAMENTAL RULES, which have no exceptions

THE PARTS OF SPEECH are formed from Root-Words by the addition of appropriate Letters.

O is the ending of the NOUN:

		ADJECTIVES end in A	
fakto	gluo	evidenta	freŝa
telefono	fajro	longa	furioza
piano	tasko	granda	simpla

NOUNS and ADJECTIVES form the PLURAL by adding J *aj, oj* sound as in *my boy*

evidentaj faktoj   longaj telefonoj   grandaj pianoj

THE SIMPLE VERB HAS ONLY SIX INFLECTIONS.

INFINITIVE	PRESENT	PAST	FUTURE	CONDITIONAL	IMPERATIVE
I	AS	IS	OS	US	U
ESTI	estas	estis	estos	estus	estu
LERNI	lernas	lernis	lernos	lernus	lernu
HELPI	helpas	helpis	helpos	helpus	helpu

N marks the ACCUSATIVE *(direct object)*
Mi *(I)* helpas lin *(him)*
Li *(he)* helpas min *(me)*
Ŝi lernas Esperanton

ADVERBS end in E
energie
entuziasme
diligente

ually thinking of religion since this everyday word incorporates a reference to God—a ridiculous misreading of a term that has lost all of its original religious significance. In like fashion, perhaps Whorf was reading too much into the Hopi lexicon and grammar, seeing significances where there were none.

The argument about how far Whorf's ideas can be stretched has gone on for several decades and promises to go on for several more. Most psychologists believe that all people see pretty much the same reality; their languages merely have different words and structures to approximate in various idiosyncratic ways a picture of that reality. And yet the experts accept what might be called modified Whorfism—a belief in the power of language to affect, if not to direct, the perception of reality. If a language is rich in terms for certain things or ideas—possesses extensive codability for them—then the people speaking that language can conceive of, and talk about, those things or ideas more conveniently. If different languages do not give their speakers entirely different world views, they certainly influence thinking to some degree.

Even within the Indo-European family of languages, some tongues have words for concepts that other tongues lack. German is especially rich in philosophical terms that have no exact counterparts in English, French, Italian—or any known language. One is "Weltschmerz," which combines in itself meanings that it takes three English phrases to adequately convey—"weariness of life," "pessimistic outlook" and "romantic discontent." Another German word that has no direct translation is "Weltanschauung." To approximate its meaning in English requires a number of different terms—"philosophy of life," "world outlook," "ideology"—for all of these elements are included in the German word. "Weltanschauung" is untranslatable into any single English term. It represents an idea for which only German has a word. Possessing the convenient term, German writers can develop this idea more easily than the users of other languages, and thus explore its ramifications further.

Even when a word from one language may seem to be easily translatable into another, it often is not really equivalent. The French term "distingué" would appear to translate easily enough into the English "distinguished." But the French use their word in ways that no English-speaker would ever employ for "distinguished." A Frenchman might reprimand his son by saying that his impolite behavior was not "distingué" or he might tell his wife that a scarf she has worn out to dinner is charmingly "distingué." The word does not mean "distinguished" as English-speakers employ the term, but something more like "suit-

Writing in the language of musical notation, the contemporary American composer Roy Harris sketches out his Père Marquette Symphony. He is using the internationally accepted staff notation, symbols that, to musicians around the world, convey the pitch and duration of notes in the same way that words convey meaning in a sentence.

able," or "appropriate" or "in keeping with polite standards." It is simply not the same word in the two languages no matter how similar the spelling. It represents a different idea, connoting a subtle difference in mental style.

In some cases the existence of a word leads users of it down tortured logical paths toward dead ends. The common word "nothing" is one example. Since there is a word for the concept, points out philosopher George Pitcher, it tempts people to think that "nothing" is a real entity, that somehow it exists, a palpable realm of not-being. It has in fact led a number of philosophers, including the French 20th Century thinker Jean-Paul Sartre, to spend a great deal of effort speculating about the nature of "nothing." The difficulty of this philosophic dilemma is indicated by a typical Sartre sentence on the subject: "The Being by which Nothingness arrives in the world must nihilate Nothingness in its Being, and even so it still runs the risk of establishing Nothingness as a transcendent in the very heart of immanence unless it nihilates Nothingness in its being *in connection with its own being*." Sartre could hardly have gotten himself tangled up in such agonized prose had French lacked a noun for "le neant," "nothing," and the value to human welfare of his attempt to explain is open to question.

The power of language to influence the world can be seen not only in comparisons of one tongue to another, but also within a single language. The way in which people use their native tongue—choosing one term over another to express the same idea or action, varying structures or phrases for different situations—has a strong effect on their attitudes toward those situations. Distasteful ideas can be made to seem acceptable or even desirable by careful choices of words, and language can make actions or beliefs that might otherwise be considered correct appear to be obsolescent or naïve. Value judgments of many kinds can be attached to seemingly simple statements. Shakespeare may have believed that "a rose by any other name would smell as sweet," but he was wrong, as other theatrical promoters have proved repeatedly. A young English vaudevillian known as Archibald Leach was a minor comedian until he was given the more romantic name of Cary Grant. The new name did not make him a star, but it did create an atmosphere in which he could demonstrate his talent, suggesting the type of character he came to exemplify.

If the power of a stage name to characterize personality seems of relatively minor consequence in human affairs, consider the effect of a different sort of appellation: "boy." It was—and sometimes still is—the form of address employed by whites in the American South in speaking to black males of any age *(page 127)*. This word, many authorities believe, served as an instrument of subjugation. It implied that the black was not a man but a child, someone not mature enough to be entrusted with responsibility for himself, let alone authority over others. His inferior position was thus made to seem natural and justified, and it could be enforced without compunction.

Characterizing people by tagging them with a word label is a worldwide practice. Many peoples use a single word to designate both themselves and the human race. "The Carib Indians, for example, have stated with no equivocation, 'We alone are people,' " reported anthropologist Jack Conrad. "Similarly, the ancient Egyptians used the word *romet* (men) only among themselves and in no case for strangers. The Lapps of Scandinavia reserve the term 'human being' for those of their own kind, while the Cherokee Indians call themselves *Ani-Yunwiya*, which means 'principal people.' The Kiowa Indians of the Southwest are willing to accept other peoples as human, but the very name, *Kiowa*, meaning 'real people,' shows their true feeling." The effect of reserving a term indicating "human" to one group is far-reaching. It alters the perception of anyone from outside that group. He is not called "human," and need not be treated as human. Like an animal, he can be entrapped, beaten or even killed with more or less impunity. This use of a word to demote whole groups from the human class is often a wartime tactic —the enemy is referred to by a pejorative name to justify killing him.

While language can be twisted to make ordinarily good things seem bad, it can also be twisted in the opposite direction to make bad things seem good or run-of-the-mill things better than they really are. The technique depends on the employment of euphemisms, a term derived from the Greek for "words of good omen." A euphemism is roundabout language that is intended to conceal something embarrassing or unpleasant. Some classes of euphemism—little evasions that people use every day —are inoffensive enough. It is when such cloudy double-talk invades the vital areas of politics and foreign affairs that it becomes perilous.

A large and commonly used—and relatively harmless—class of euphemism has to do with bodily functions. Many people shy away from frank talk about excretion or sex; in fact, many of the old, vivid terms —the four-letter words—are socially taboo. So people for centuries have skirted the edge of such matters, inventing a rich vocabulary of substitute terms. Americans offered turkey on Thanksgiving commonly say "white meat" or "dark meat" to announce their preference. These terms date back to the 19th Century when it was considered indelicate to say

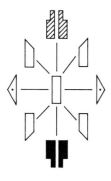

Labanotation records dance movements on an eight-column "staff" divided into right and left sides. Each column represents a part of the body—except the center pair, which stands for parts of the body a dancer uses to support weight. In practice, only three lines separating columns (heavy lines) are drawn.

Symbols (left) are placed on the staff (above) to show the direction a part of the body is moved. The rectangle represents the movement of a part of the body "into place"—along the body's vertical axis. Bottle-shaped figures at top and bottom indicate forward and backward movement. Triangles indicate movement right or left, and the four slanted figures diagonal movement. Cross-hatching, dots or shadings call for movement up, horizontally or down.

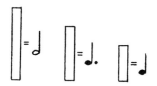

The duration of each movement is indicated by the length of the symbol. These rectangles mean the body part moves into place, taking the same amount of time as the musical equivalents alongside them (left to right): two beats, one and a half beats and one beat.

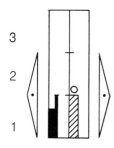

All three elements of Laban's dance language are combined in this example. The hatched area shows that the dancer rises in place on his right foot. The shaded bottle shape indicates the left leg moving forward, low. Triangles with dots mean arms moving to the sides horizontally. Numbers mark off beats —the left leg and right foot occupying one beat, the arms taking two beats.

Dancer Jean Erdman leaps and twists across

The dictionary of the dance

the floor in a series of complex movements that are recorded in the notation at right.

A sequence of dance steps, illustrated by the multiple exposure at left, is recorded in the Labanotation below. Reading from the bottom up, the tightly compressed symbols utilize the method explained on the opposite page to express the action in a compact, readily readable language.

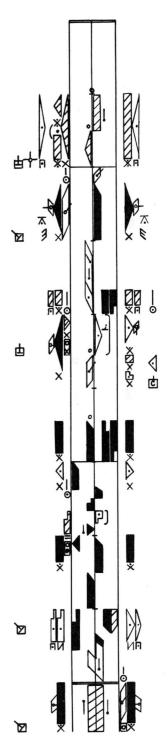

The sensation of the Paris ballet in 1913 was *Le Sacre du Printemps*, choreographed by the great Russian dancer Nijinsky. But no one today can say precisely what the dancing was like. Nijinsky's choreography for the opening performance is now lost, for there was no accepted way of recording the complexities of human movement. For centuries the great dances and ballets had to be kept alive by memory, and choreographers planning new performances had to rely on their recollections of steps and routines. As a result, whole ballets were forgotten.

All this is changing, thanks to several notation systems. One of the most widely used is Labanotation, devised by a Hungarian-born teacher, Rudolf von Laban, in 1928. It uses symbols, as shown here, to identify each part of the body that moves, its direction and its timing. This system and others seem complex to the uninitiated, but choreographers and dance teachers can read them, and they are gaining international recognition primarily as ways to preserve choreography after it has been created. Eventually, many experts believe, such notation might enable dance masters to compose ballets in writing, just as music is composed.

"breast" or "leg." "Toilet," itself a euphemism coined from the French "toilette" ("making oneself presentable to the outside world"), long ago became tainted and too graphic for the prudish. The list of euphemistic substitutes is almost endless, ranging from the commonplace "washroom," "bathroom" and "restroom" (whoever rests in a restroom?) to "john," "head" and "Chic Sale" in the United States, and in England "the loo." "Loo" may be derived from a mistaken English pronunciation of the French "l'eau," "water." Or it may be a euphemism derived from a euphemism. The French, with Gallic delicacy, once commonly put the number 100 on bathroom doors in hotels. It is easy to see how an English person might have mistaken the number for the word "loo." Meanwhile, ladies in restaurants have adopted "I'm going to powder my nose" or, in England, where it once cost a penny to use public toilets, "I'm going to spend a penny."

Another generally harmless use of euphemistic language is the practice, especially notable in the United States, of giving prestigious names to more-or-less ordinary trades. As H. L. Mencken pointed out in *The American Language*, his masterly examination of English as spoken in the United States, ratcatchers are fond of calling themselves "exterminating engineers" and hairdressers have long since showed a preference for "beautician." The *-ician* ending, in fact, has proved very popular, doubtless because it echoes "physician" and thus sounds both professional and scientific. In the late 19th Century undertakers had already begun to call themselves "funeral directors," but starting in 1916 ennobled themselves even further by battening on the newer euphemistic coinage, "mortician." Meanwhile a tree trimmer became a "tree surgeon" (that love of medicine again) and a press agent became a "publicist" or, even more grandly, a "public relations counsel."

Americans (and the English, too) not only chose high-sounding euphemisms for their professions but also gave new and gaudy names to their places of business. Thus pawn shops became "loan offices," saloons became "cocktail rooms," pool halls became "billiard parlors" and barber shops "hair-styling salons."

Purists might say that such shading or blunting of the stark truth leads to moral decay, but it is difficult to see why anybody should be the worse for allowing women to excuse themselves by pleading that they must powder their noses. There are euphemisms, however, that are clearly anything but harmless. These are evasive, beclouding phraseologies that hide truths people must clearly perceive if they are to govern themselves intelligently and keep a check on those in positions of power. Slick phrases, slippery evasions—words deliberately designed to hide unpleasant truth rather than reveal it—can so becloud political processes and so easily hide mistaken policies that the entire health of a nation is imperiled.

The classic treatise on the political misuse of language in modern times is the 1946 essay "Politics and the English Language" by the British writer George Orwell. "In our time, political speech and writing are largely the defence of the indefensible," Orwell said. "Thus political language has to consist largely of euphemism, question-begging and sheer cloudy vagueness." He concluded, "Such phraseology is needed if one wants to name things without calling up mental pictures of them. . . . When there is a gap between one's real and one's declared aims, one turns as it were instinctively to long words and exhausted idioms, like a cuttlefish squirting out ink."

Orwell supplied numerous examples to buttress his charges. "Defenceless villages are bombarded from the air, the inhabitants driven out into the countryside, the cattle machine-gunned, the huts set on fire with incendiary bullets: this is called *pacification*." He went on to observe that in Stalin's Russia people were "imprisoned for years without trial or shot in the back of the neck or sent to die of scurvy in Arctic lumber camps: this is called *elimination of unreliable elements*."

Orwell, who died at the age of 46 in 1950, did not live to collect even

The language of the cosmos

If inhabitants of earth cannot find a common tongue, how could they communicate with intelligent beings from other planets? The answer—from Carl Sagan of Cornell University, who with his wife, Linda, designed the "space postcard" *(right)* sent aboard Pioneer 10—was to use symbols of physics, mathematics and astronomy.

The key is the diagram identifying the hydrogen atom *(top left)*, whose universally recognizable characteristics yield length and time measures to differentiate the sun from 14 stars around it *(center)*. The bottom diagram plots sun and planets—indicating the third one out as home to Pioneer and the creatures in front of its outline.

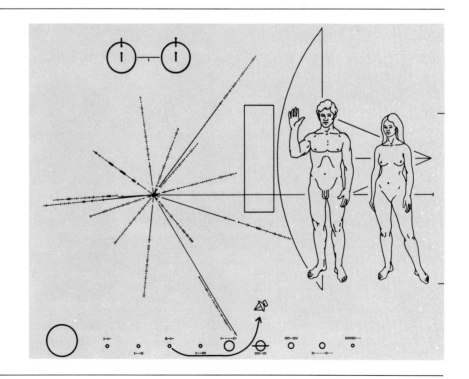

The euphemism down the hall

Of all euphemisms—inoffensive words that substitute for terms deemed impolite—the commonest and strangest are those used for "toilet," itself a euphemism *(page 156)*. Although there are plenty of old terms, new ones are constantly being invented, particularly, it seems, by restaurant owners driven to find whimsical words distinguishing the men's toilet from the women's.

The words labeling the appropriate doors may reach for Biblical allegory, as in "Adam" and "Eve," barnyard analogy ("roosters" and "hens") or, as observed in one seashore clam bar, puns ("buoys" and "gulls"). Others utilize the ultimate in understatement, the wordless emblems that are shown on these pages.

This pictorial euphemism for the euphemism "men's and women's rooms" is from a German tavern. Those opposite are labeled with the countries where they are found. All have been understood save for the biological signs (bottom right): the figures were added after a period of confusion proved them necessary.

FINLAND

UNITED STATES

FRANCE

ITALY

SPAIN

GREECE

more deplorable distortions of language. The French clothed their brutal war in Algeria with a veil of euphemism; the North Koreans accused the South Koreans of "aggression" when the North invaded the South. The United States invented a whole lexicon of gobblydegook to disguise the horror of the war in Vietnam: "protective reaction strike" (the bombing of a Vietnamese village); "surgical bombing" (the same as protective reaction strike); "free-fire zone" (an area in which troops could shoot anything that moved, including helpless villagers); "new life hamlet" (a refugee camp for survivors of a surgical bombing).

Perhaps the most appalling use of this type of euphemism was the word employed by the Nazis for their program to exterminate all of Europe's Jews. The word is "Endlösung," which means final solution. Behind that verbal façade the Nazis gassed, burned, shot or worked to death some six million Jews from Germany, France, Poland and other conquered parts of Europe. Hitler and Gestapo chief Himmler often employed the euphemism among themselves, and it was always used in official records—but not necessarily to preserve secrecy for purposes of state security. Apparently the euphemism shielded the Nazis from themselves. Openly brutal and murderous as they were, they could not face up to the horrible reality of what they were doing, and they had to hide it in innocuous language.

Such distortion of language can do more than disguise truth. It can turn truth around, so that the idea conveyed is the opposite of actuality. After the U.S.S.R. savagely crushed the Hungarian rebellion in 1956 the Soviet aggression was made to seem, in the twisted language used by other Communist dictatorships, an expression of friendship. The Peking radio commented after the rebellion was put down: "The Hungarian people can see that Soviet policy toward the people's democracies is truly one of equality, friendship and mutual assistance, not of conquest, aggression and plunder."

The possibility that such topsy-turvy language might ultimately make the world topsy-turvy—an ironic demonstration of the fundamental truth of Benjamin Lee Whorf's insights—was raised in a dramatic way by George Orwell. His novel *1984*, a chilling and convincing description of life in a totalitarian society, shows how language might destroy reality. In the imaginary nation of Oceania the official language is Newspeak, which is intended to facilitate "doublethink," the ability to accept simultaneously ideas contradicting each other. The Oceania state apparatus includes a Ministry of Truth, its headquarters building emblazoned with three slogans: "WAR IS PEACE"; "FREEDOM IS SLAVERY"; "IGNORANCE IS STRENGTH." There are also other ministries, Orwell explained: "The Ministry of Peace, which concerned itself with war; the Ministry of Love, which maintained law and order." Anyone who would use language this way, Orwell made clear, denies the meaning of his words. He has lost touch with reality and substituted for it an emptiness concealed in sounds that once had meaning.

There is another threat to language beside the intentional twisting of words by demagogues and others who would control men's thoughts. It is less obvious, but a danger nevertheless: simple imprecision, slovenliness, mindlessness in the use of the language. It seems a small matter that English-speakers increasingly confuse "uninterested" with "disinterested," for example. But these words do not mean the same thing. "Disinterested" means "impartial," "not taking sides." "Uninterested" means "lacking in interest," "bored." A judge should be "disinterested" but never "uninterested." Many such changes result from the inevitable evolution of language as it changes over the years, but the change can be a loss. The slow erosion of distinctions, visible in much writing, audible in many conversations, makes language imprecise and thus clumsy and ineffective as communication.

Among the symptoms of such erosion are stock phrases that people mindlessly repeat, substituting noise for thought. Everyone has heard speechmakers use such clichés as "having regard to," "play into the hands of," "in the interest of," "no ax to grind." Although this brief list is drawn from Orwell's essay of 1946 these exhausted clichés are still heard. Such verbal dead limbs do not distort thought but rather tend to obliterate it in a cloud of meaninglessness. "The slovenliness of our language makes it easier for us to have foolish thoughts," wrote Orwell. And ultimately, as has been pointed out by commentator Edwin Newman in his book *Strictly Speaking*, "Those for whom words have lost their value are likely to find that ideas have also lost their value."

The masters of persuasion

One of the great powers of language lies in its capacity, when expertly handled, to persuade and convince. Through history eloquence has—for better or for worse—moved men to political action, even to fight and die for a cause, and those gifted with great skill at oratory have controlled the flow of events.

The art of persuasion through words was long called "rhetoric." The term in modern times has picked up negative connotations, suggesting contrived but meaningless words used for manipulative purposes. But to Aristotle, who first defined rhetoric, it was a high road to truth and good—the way a democratic society's leaders presented their ideas and rallied the people to decisive action. Aristotle believed that three things were needed for successful rhetoric: the character of the speaker had to be forceful and convincing; his arguments had to be presented logically; his rapport with his listeners had to be highly developed—that is, he had to understand their psychology, sense their emotional state and select the words that would best appeal to those emotions.

The spellbinders of history have lived up to Aristotle's definition. Some, like Sir Winston Churchill *(page 165)*, have been most adept at ringing phrases. Others, like Adolf Hitler *(page 167)* or Fidel Castro *(opposite)*, have been mesmerizing talkers who held forth at great length and with great effectiveness before mass audiences. But all of them have possessed Aristotle's three abilities, in one proportion or another, and through their expert use of rhetoric have changed the world.

Cuba's Premier Fidel Castro, gesturing broadly, addresses a political rally in Havana in 1960, a year after he overthrew the Batista dictatorship. A fervid orator, he can keep an audience attentive for three hours, frequently joking with them and evoking their responses. But his speeches are not merely emotional. Using notes, he lards his talks with facts arranged logically—and persuasively.

The phrasemakers

Some speakers have possessed an uncanny ability to coin the perfect phrase that stirs men to action and is remembered for all time. They have tuned language to its utmost pitch, electrifying their audiences through the power of their words. Three of history's greatest phrasemakers were Patrick Henry, the 18th Century American patriot; William Jennings Bryan, the turn-of-the-century American politician; and Britain's World War II Prime Minister, Sir Winston Churchill. Probably the greatest was Churchill, who, thundering defiance in one great speech after another, rallied the British people to fight alone in 1940 against the terrible might of Nazi Germany.

Bryan, the grandiloquent phrasemaker, delivers one of the 600 speeches he made as a Presidential candidate in 1896. He had been nominated after delivering one of history's most effective speeches. Urging that the nation abandon scarce gold as the basis of its currency and substitute silver, thus aiding the poor through a more plentiful supply of money, Bryan summed up his address by fulminating, "You shall not crucify mankind upon a cross of gold."

Churchill addresses the crew of the cruiser Exeter in February 1940 after it helped rout the German Graf Spee. With a few such small victories and rattling phrases in several speeches that spring —"I have nothing to offer but blood, toil, tears, and sweat"; "We shall fight on the beaches, we shall fight on the landing grounds"; "'This was their finest hour'"—Churchill rallied a nation.

Young Patrick Henry, a firebrand patriot, urges his fellow Virginians to arm against British oppression in 1775. He concluded his magnificent speech with the flaming lines: "Is life so dear, or peace so sweet, as to be purchased at the price of chains and slavery? Forbid it, Almighty God! I know not what course others may take. But as for me— give me liberty or give me death!"

The 15th Century Italian monk Girolamo Savonarola causes the people of Florence to weep and shudder as he attacks them for their sins. Playing upon their fear of damnation, he drove them to burn paintings, books and other "vanities."

Maximilien Robespierre, as always ramrod straight and immaculately dressed, delivers one of his orations at the Jacobin Club during the French Revolution. He triggered the French people's anger by telling them that traitors were trying to subvert the Revolution. He made the systematic use of terror seem logical, and thousands of suspects were guillotined.

The rabblerousers

Aristotle specified that the truly effective speaker must understand the way his audience thinks and feels. Two of the most powerful emotions, he went on, are hatred and fear. Aristotle did not foresee the evil uses demagogues through history would make of his advice, manipulating people by playing on their fears and hatreds.

Perhaps the most fiendishly effective was Germany's dictator Adolf Hitler *(below)*, who rose to power by convincing the German people that they were surrounded by enemies. He so aroused their anxieties and angers that they followed him into disaster.

Fist clenched and face contorted, Hitler harangues his followers in 1932. Preaching hatred of France, Russia and other nations, he also appealed to the Germans' anti-Semitism. Said an observer: "He started as a soapbox orator and spoke his way to power."

The personalities

The character of a leader, Aristotle said, "may almost be called the most effective means of persuasion he possesses." The national leaders who are pictured here—Russia's Nikolai Lenin, France's Charles de Gaulle, America's Franklin D. Roosevelt—were men of immense personal force. Their speeches were artful, but it was their personal magnetism that won over their listeners. All were able through their words and their towering authority to persuade their respective nations to follow them along new paths in times of crisis.

Perhaps de Gaulle was the most mesmeric of the three leaders; he convinced many of his compatriots that he was not only France's leader, but the nation's spirit incarnate.

Lenin, who embodied the spirit of the Russian Revolution, addresses an outdoor meeting in Moscow in 1917. His effectiveness stemmed, said one observer, from "an impression of ruthless integrity." As a result he gave people the feeling that he was invincible.

President de Gaulle, standing before huge initials for République Française, urges the French to adopt a new 1958 constitution. De Gaulle's deep voice, his stately dignity and the nobility of his style combined to convince the French that he could restore the country to former glory.

"The only thing we have to fear is fear itself," said President Roosevelt in 1933, and Depression-battered Americans believed in him.

*Dr. Martin Luther King, the charismatic
leader of the 1960s movement to bring
full equality to American blacks,
addresses the 200,000 demonstrators who
marched on Washington, D.C., in 1963.
King embodied the gifts Aristotle felt
were needed for great rhetoric. He had
personal charm and understood the hopes
of his audience. His arguments were
clear, forceful and eloquent. It was in
Washington that he announced: "I have
a dream that my four little children will
one day live in a nation where they will
not be judged by the color of their skin."*

Acknowledgments

The authors and editors of this book are particularly indebted to Professor Sam Glucksberg, Department of Psychology, Princeton University, Princeton, New Jersey. They also wish to thank the following persons and institutions: Professor Asen Balikci, Department of Anthropology, University of Montreal, Montreal, Canada; Ray L. Birdwhistell, Professor of Communications, University of Pennsylvania, Philadelphia; Rand Castile, The Japan Society, New York City; Professor James Cathey, Department of Germanic Languages, University of Massachusetts, Amherst; Dance Notation Bureau, New York City; Peter A. Eddy, Center for Applied Linguistics, Arlington, Virginia; Professor Roger Fouts, Department of Psychology, University of Oklahoma, Norman; R. M. R. Hall, Associate Professor of Linguistics, Queens College, New York City; Paul Koasak, Invit Tapirisat (Eskimo Brotherhood), Ottawa, Ontario, Canada; William Myers, Office of Facilitation, United States Department of Transportation, Washington, D.C.; Genevieve Oswald, Curator of the Dance Collection of the New York Public Library, New York City; Joseph M. Sorce Jr., Harwood Heights, Illinois; Ethel Strainchamps, New York City.

Bibliography

Bauman, Richard, and Joel Sherzer, eds., *Explorations in the Ethnography of Speaking*. Cambridge University Press, 1974.

Berkowitz, Leonard, ed., *Advances in Experimental Social Psychology*. Vol. 4. Academic Press, 1970.

Birdwhistell, Ray L., *Kinesics and Context*. University of Pennsylvania Press, 1970.

Birket-Smith, Kaj, *Eskimos*. Crown Publishers, Inc., 1971.

Bowerman, Melissa, *Early Syntactic Development*. Cambridge University Press, 1973.

Brown, Roger:
A First Language. Harvard University Press, 1973.
ed., *Psycholinguistics*. The Free Press, 1972.
Social Psychology. The Free Press, 1965.
Words and Things. The Free Press, 1958.

Brown, Roger, and Richard J. Herrnstein, *Psychology*. Little, Brown & Co., 1975.

Bruemmer, Fred, *Seasons of the Eskimo*. McClelland and Stewart Limited, 1971.

Carroll, John B., ed., *Language, Thought and Reality: Selected Writings of Benjamin Lee Whorf*. M.I.T. Press, 1956.

Chomsky, Noam:
"A Review of Verbal Behavior." *Language*, Vol. 35 (1959), pp. 26-58.
Language and Mind. Harcourt Brace Jovanovich, Inc., 1972.
Syntactic Structures. Humanities Press, Inc., 1957.

Christie, Richard, and Florence L. Geis, *Studies in Machiavellianism*. Academic Press, 1970.

Conrad, Jack, *The Many Worlds of Man*. Thomas Y. Crowell Company, 1964.

Dale, Philip S., *Language Development*. The Dryden Press, Inc., 1972.

Deese, James, *Psycholinguistics*. Allyn and Bacon, Inc., 1970.

Denes, Peter, and Elliot Pinson, *The Speech Chain*. Anchor Books, 1973.

Dillard, J. L.:
Black English. Vintage Books, 1973.
All-American English. Random House, 1975.

Dubin, Joseph, *The Green Star*. National Institute of Esperanto, 1944.

Ekman, Paul, and W. V. Friesen, "The Repertoire of Nonverbal Behavior: Categories, Origins, Usage, and Coding." *Semiotica* 1 (1969), pp. 49-98.

Farb, Peter, *Word Play*. Alfred A. Knopf, 1974.

Glucksberg, Sam, and Joseph H. Danks, *Experimental Psycholinguistics*. Lawrence Erlbaum Associates, Publishers, 1975.

Goffman, Erving, *Behavior in Public Places*. The Free Press, 1966.

Goldman, Albert, and Lawrence Schiller, *Ladies and Gentlemen Lenny Bruce!!* Ballantine Books, 1974.

Hall, Edward T:
The Hidden Dimension. Anchor Books, 1969.
The Silent Language. Doubleday & Company, Inc., 1959.

Hass, Hans, *The Human Animal*. G. P. Putnam's Sons, 1970.

Jacobs, Noah J., *Naming-Day in Eden*. The Macmillan Company, 1958.

Jennings, Gary, *Personalities of Language*. Thomas Y. Crowell Company, 1965.

Keller, Helen, *The Story of My Life*. Dell Publishing Co., Inc., 1974.

Knapp, Mark L., *Nonverbal Communication in Human Interaction*. Holt, Rinehart & Winston, Inc., 1972.

Krauss, Robert M., "Language as a Symbolic Process in Communication." *American Scientist*, Vol. 56, No. 3 (Autumn 1968), pp. 265-278.

Labov, William:
Language in the Inner City. University of Pennsylvania Press, 1972.
Sociolinguistic Patterns. University of Pennsylvania Press, 1972.

Lindzey, Gardner, and E. Aronson, *Handbook of Social Psychology*. Addison-Wesley Publishing Company, Inc., 1968.

McKeon, Richard, ed., *The Basic Works of Aristotle*. Random House, 1941.

Mencken, H. L., *The American Language*. Alfred A. Knopf, 1961.

Mitford, Nancy, ed., *Noblesse Oblige.* Hamish Hamilton Ltd., 1956.

Nash, Walter, *Our Experience of Language.* St. Martin's Press, 1971.

Newman, Edwin, *Strictly Speaking.* The Bobbs-Merrill Company, Inc., 1974.

Orwell, George, *Shooting an Elephant.* Harcourt Brace Jovanovich, Inc., 1950.

Pei, Mario:
The Story of Language. Mentor Books, 1966.
Words in Sheep's Clothing. Hawthorn Books, Inc., 1969.

Piaget, Jean, and Bärbel Inhelder, *The Psychology of the Child.* Basic Books, Inc., 1969.

Pitcher, George, *The Philosophy of Wittgenstein.* Prentice-Hall, Inc., 1964.

Platz, Mabel, ed., *Anthology of Public Speeches.* The H. W. Wilson Company, 1940.

Reisner, Robert, *Graffiti: Two Thousand Years of Wall Writing.* Cowles Book Company, 1971.

Robinson, W. P., *Language and Social Behavior.* Penguin Books, 1972.

Rosenthal, Robert, and Lenore Jacobson, *Pygmalion in the Classroom.* Holt, Rinehart & Winston, Inc., 1968.

Samarin, William, *Tongues of Men and Angels.* The Macmillan Company, 1972.

Scheflen, Albert E., *Body Language and Social Order.* Prentice-Hall, Inc., 1972.

Sebeok, Thomas A., ed., *Style in Language.* M.I.T. Press, 1971.

Slobin, Dan I., *Psycholinguistics.* Scott, Foresman & Company, 1971.

Steiner, George, *After Babel.* Oxford University Press, 1975.

Williams, Frederick, ed., *Language and Poverty.* Markham Publishing Company, 1971.

Picture Credits

Sources for illustrations (credits from left to right are separated by semicolons, from top to bottom by dashes):

Cover—James H. Karales. 6—Friedrich Rauch courtesy Juliane Roh, taken from the book *Photo-Eye* edited by Franz Roh and Jan Tschichold. 10,11—Franz Goës from TIME-LIFE Picture Agency. 15 —Roger Fouts. 17—CBS. 18,19—Courtesy Office of Facilitation, United States Department of Transportation. 21—Margaret Bourke-White from TIME-LIFE Picture Agency. 23—Chart reproduced with permission. From *Webster's New World Dictionary*, College Edition. Copyright © 1968 by The World Publishing Company. 25—Courtesy The Thomas Gilcrease Institute of American History and Art, Tulsa, Oklahoma. 26,27—Willy François from TIME-LIFE Picture Agency. 30 through 41—Stefan Moses. 42—Wolf von dem Bussche. 45—Dominique Berretty from Rapho Guillumette. 48—Ken Heyman. 51—© Walt Disney Productions—© Asterix: *La Serpe d'Or*, Dargaud Editeur —© Walt Disney Productions. 52—Steve Schapiro. 55—Courtesy American Foundation for the Blind. 56—Courtesy American Foundation for the Blind; Courtesy Alexander Graham Bell Association for the Deaf. 57,58—Courtesy American Foundation for the Blind. 61—Gene Laurents. 62—Dick Davis from TIME-LIFE Picture Agency. 64—Jill Krementz. 67 —Janine Niepce from Rapho/Photo Researchers. 68—Jochen Blume. 71—The Bettmann Archive. 74,75—Ted Spiegel. 78,79—Gene Laurents. 81—© Julio Mitchel. 82—Laurence B. Fink. 83—Laurence B. Fink—Gary Freedman from Jeroboam. 85—Thomas Höpker from Woodfin Camp and Associates. 87—Marc Riboud from Magnum. 90—René Burri. 92—The Bettmann Archive. 93—Culver Pictures except lower right, Courtesy International Museum of Photography at George Eastman House. 96,97,98—Henri Cartier-Bresson from Magnum. 99—George Krause —Martine Franck from Woodfin Camp and Associates. 100,101—Marvin Koner; Roger Malloch from Magnum. 102 —Charles Harbutt from Magnum—United Press International. 103—Donald McCullin from Magnum. 104,105—Bruno Mooser (3); Ted Spiegel. 106,107 —Thomas Höpker from Woodfin Camp and Associates. 108—Copyright Moldvay, Stern. 112—Baldev Pix. 114,115—Leif Skoogfors from Woodfin Camp and Associates—Sepp Seitz from Magnum; Brian Seed. 117—Leonard McCombe from TIME-LIFE Picture Agency. 120 —Fred Conrad. 122—Robert W. Kelley from TIME-LIFE Picture Agency. 123 —Drawing by Dana Fradon, © 1975 The New Yorker Magazine, Inc. 125—Fox Photos Ltd., London. 129—Syndication International. 132—Charles Harbutt from Magnum. 134—David Sim courtesy The Observer. 136—Gene Laurents. 139 —Frank Lerner. 140,141—Fred Bruemmer. 144—Leonard Freed from Magnum. 145—Charles Biasiny. 148—Brown Brothers; Chart courtesy Esperanto Association of North America. 150,151—William Gedney. 154,155—Left drawings, no credit; Walter Daran; Drawing by Dance Notation Bureau, Inc. 157—Drawing by NASA. 159—Top row, Suomen Kuvapalvelu Oy (2); Gene Laurents (2)—Middle row, Roger-Viollet (2); Alto Durazzi (2)—Bottom row, Marco Schiavo (2); Kimon Raphaelidis (2). 162,163—Lynn Pehlam from Rapho/Photo Researchers. 164—The Bettmann Archive. 165—TIME-LIFE Picture Agency —The Bettmann Archive. 166,167—The Bettmann Archive; Culver Pictures —Courtesy Stefan Lorant. 168—The Bettmann Archive—Loomis Dean from TIME-LIFE Picture Agency. 169—United Press International. 170,171—Gordon Parks from TIME-LIFE Picture Agency.

Index

Numerals in italics indicate a photograph or drawing of the subject mentioned.

Printed in U.S.A.